BEING A
WRITER

BEING A
WRITER

**ADVICE, MUSINGS, ESSAYS AND EXPERIENCES
FROM THE WORLD'S GREATEST AUTHORS**

**TRAVIS ELBOROUGH
HELEN GORDON**

ILLUSTRATIONS BY JOEY GUIDONE

I want to do something splendid . . .
Something heroic or wonderful that
won't be forgotten after I'm dead . . .
I think I shall write books.
Louisa May Alcott

6 .... Introduction

9 .... Becoming a writer
Finding your way

51 .... Methods and means
Getting down to it

111 .... Failing
Writer's block and other troubles

153 .... The art of writing
Searching for words

207 .... A sense of an ending
Drawing conclusions

224 .... Sources
232 .... Index of authors
234 .... Subject index
236 .... Acknowledgments

Introduction

Start work at dawn/9 A.M./midnight. Write with a felt-tip pen/ an Olivetti Lettera 22/a slimline Apple Mac. Work at your kitchen table/in a sound-proofed office/on a crowded train.

Compiling this book, it quickly became obvious that there's not one correct way to go about the business of writing. It's a liberating thought. For every novelist who needs to isolate themselves in a quiet office (Jonathan Franzen), there's another who works best over tea and cookies at the local coffee shop (Rivka Galchen) or who struggles to snatch an hour between chores and when the children are sleeping (a young Alice Munro). Anthony Trollope began writing at 5.30 A.M. every morning and paid an elderly groom £5 a year to act as an alarm clock; for H.P. Lovecraft only the 'magical and quiet' night-world ushered in the necessary inspiration.

Conversely, it also became apparent that alongside all this variety of approach there are certain ideas, certain pieces of advice, which many writers hold in common. In an 1866 letter to Mrs Brookfield, Charles Dickens suggests that: 'you constantly hurry your narrative . . . by telling it, in a sort of impetuous breathless way, in your own person, when the people [characters] should tell it and act it for themselves.' Basically: SHOW DON'T TELL. Three words that will be familiar to anyone who has sat in a twenty-first-century creative writing class. And among the contemporary writers one of the more popular pieces of advice was simple: *Turn off the Wi-Fi!*

We hope that there's much here to inspire and delight, including Raymond Carver on finding inspiration in everyday lives; Herman Melville on the importance of a great theme; Ernest Hemingway's method for avoiding writer's block; David Mitchell on how to approach agents and editors; and F. Scott Fitzgerald on what can be written while drinking (a short story) and what can't (a novel). Writers talk about what went wrong as well as what went right. They discuss failing to finish a manuscript, failing to find a publisher, badly realised characters and tortuous, unwieldy plots. Sitting alone in front of a blank computer screen or empty notebook it can help to be reminded that other people, those writers one most admires, in fact, have faced some of the same challenges and struggles. 'Every time I try to start a novel I feel like I've never written one before,' says Franzen.

This book is not intended as a comprehensive survey but it is wide-angled. From Samuel Johnson in eighteenth-century London to Lorrie Moore in twenty-first-century Wisconsin, *Being a Writer* covers more than 250 years and features novelists and short-story writers from, among other places, Spain, Japan, Nigeria, Germany, France, Australia, Switzerland, South Korea and Argentina. It attempts to explore and illuminate the pleasures and pitfalls of the compulsion to write. As George Orwell puts it: 'From a very early age . . . I knew that when I grew up I should be a writer. . . . Between the ages of about seventeen and twenty-four I tried to abandon this idea, but I did so with the consciousness that I was outraging my true nature and that sooner or later I should have to settle down and write books.'

BECOMING A WRITER

Finding your way

When the question is therefore asked, 'Are writers born or made?' one should first ask, 'Do you mean writers of talent or writers of originality?' Because everybody can write but not everybody invents new forms of writing. Gertrude Stein invented new forms of writing and her imitators are just 'talents'.

Jack Kerouac

Now I absolutely flatly deny that I am a soul, or a body, or a mind, or an intelligence, or a brain, or a nervous system, or a bunch of glands, or any of the rest of these bits of me. The whole is greater than the part. And therefore, I who am man alive, am greater than my soul, or spirit, or body, or mind, or consciousness, or anything else that is merely a part of me. I am a man, and alive. I am man alive, and as long as I can, I intend to go on being man-alive.

For this reason I am a novelist. And being a novelist, I consider myself superior to the saint, the scientist, the philosopher, and the poet, who are all great masters of different bits of man-alive, but never get the whole hog.

The novel is the one bright book of life. Books are not life. They are only tremulations on the ether. But the novel as a tremulation can make the whole man alive tremble. Which is more than poetry, philosophy, science, or any other book-tremulation *can* do.

D.H. Lawrence

Mark Twain

When I was sixteen or seventeen years old, a splendid idea burst upon me – a bran-new one, which had never occurred to anybody before: I would write some 'pieces' and take them down to the editor of the 'Republican', and ask him to give me his plain, unvarnished opinion of their value! Now, as old and threadbare as the idea was, it was fresh and beautiful to me, and it went flaming and crashing through my system like the genuine lightning and thunder of originality. I wrote the pieces. I wrote them with that placid confidence and that happy facility which only want of practice and absence of literary experience can give. There was not one sentence in them that cost half an hour's weighing and shaping and trimming and fixing. Indeed, it is possible that there was no one sentence whose mere wording cost even one-sixth of that time. If I remember rightly, there was not one single erasure or interlineation in all that chaste manuscript. (I have since lost that large belief in my powers, and likewise that marvellous perfection of execution.) I started down to the 'Republican' office with my pocket full of manuscripts, my brain full of dreams, and a grand future opening out before me. I knew perfectly well that the editor would be ravished with my pieces. But presently –

However, the particulars are of no consequence. I was only about to say that a shadowy sort of doubt just then intruded upon my exaltation. Another came, and another. Pretty soon a whole procession of them. And at last, when I stood before the 'Republican' office and looked up at its tall, unsympathetic front, it seemed hardly *me* that could have 'chinned' its towers ten minutes before, and was now so shrunk up and pitiful that if I dared to step on the gratings I should probably go through.

At about that crisis the editor, the very man I had come to consult, came down stairs, and halted a moment to pull at his wristbands and settle his coat to its place, and he happened to notice that I was eyeing him wistfully. He asked me what I wanted. I answered, 'NOTHING!' with a boy's own meekness and shame; and, dropping my eyes, crept humbly round till I was fairly in the alley, and then drew a big grateful breath of relief, and picked up my heels and ran!

I was satisfied. I wanted no more. It was my first attempt to get a 'plain unvarnished opinion' out of a literary man concerning my compositions, and it has lasted me until now.

My father said I was the ugliest child he had ever seen. He told me that all my life and I believed him. And I'd accepted that nobody would ever love me. But do you know, nobody cares what a writer looks like. I could write to be eighty and be as grotesque as a dwarf and that wouldn't matter. For me, writing was an act of love. It was an attempt to get the world's attention, it was an attempt to be loved. It seemed to me a way to save myself and to save my family. It came out of despair. And it seemed the only way into another world.

James Baldwin

I asked for and was given a notebook and a bottle of purple ink. I inscribed on the cover: 'Novel Notebook'. The first story I completed was entitled *For a Butterfly*. A scientist, his daughter, and an athletic young explorer sailed up the Amazon in search of a precious butterfly. The argument, the characters, the particulars of the adventures, and even the title were borrowed from a story in pictures that had appeared in the preceding quarter. This cold-blooded plagiarism freed me from my remaining misgivings; everything was necessarily true since I invented nothing. I did not aspire to be published, but I had contrived to be printed in advance, and I did not pen a line that was not guaranteed by my model. Did I take myself for an imitator? No, but for an original author. I retouched, I livened things up. For example, I was careful to change the names of the characters. This slight tampering entitled me to blend memory and imagination. New sentences, already written, took shape in my head with the implacable sureness ascribed to inspiration. I transcribed them. They took on, beneath my eyes, the density of things. If, as is commonly believed, the inspired author is other than himself in the depths of his soul, I experienced inspiration between the ages of seven and eight.

I was never completely taken in by this 'automatic writing'. But I also enjoyed the game for its own sake. Being an only child, I could play it by myself. Now and then I would stop writing. I would pretend to hesitate, I would pucker my brow, assume a moonstruck expression, so as to feel I was a writer.

Jean-Paul Sartre

Perhaps it is just as well to be rash and foolish for a while. If writers were too wise, perhaps no books would be written at all. It might be better to ask yourself 'Why?' afterwards than before. Anyway, the force from somewhere in space which commands you to write in the first place, gives you no choice. You take up the pen when you are told, and write what is commanded.

Zora Neale Hurston

How vain it is to sit down and write when you have not stood up to live.
Henry David Thoreau

The impulse to write things down is a peculiarly compulsive one, inexplicable to those who do not share it, useful only accidentally, only secondarily, in the way that any compulsion tries to justify itself. I suppose that it begins or does not begin in the cradle. Although I have felt compelled to write things down since I was five years old, I doubt that my daughter ever will, for she is a singularly blessed and accepting child, delighted with life exactly as life presents itself to her, unafraid to go to sleep and unafraid to wake up. Keepers of private notebooks are a different breed altogether, lonely and resistant rearrangers of things, anxious malcontents, children afflicted apparently at birth with some presentiment of loss.

My first notebook was a Big Five tablet, given to me by my mother with the sensible suggestion that I stop whining and learn to amuse myself by writing down my thoughts. She returned the tablet to me a few years ago; the first entry is an account of a woman who believed herself to be freezing to death in the Arctic night, only to find, when day broke, that she had stumbled onto the Sahara Desert, where she would die of the heat before lunch. I have no idea what turn of a five-year-old's mind could have prompted so insistently 'ironic' and exotic a story, but it does reveal a certain predilection for the extreme which has dogged me into adult life; perhaps if I were analytically inclined I would find it a truer story than any I might have told about Donald Johnson's birthday party or the day my cousin Brenda put Kitty Litter in the aquarium.

Joan Didion

Colette

To write is to pour one's innermost self
passionately upon the tempting paper, at
such frantic speed that sometimes one's
hand struggles and rebels, overdriven by the
impatient god who guides it – and to find,
next day, in place of the golden bough that
boomed miraculously in that dazzling hour,
a withered bramble and a stunted flower.

George Orwell

From a very early age, perhaps the age of five or six, I knew that when I grew up I should be a writer. Between the ages of about seventeen and twenty-four I tried to abandon this idea, but I did so with the consciousness that I was outraging my true nature and that sooner or later I should have to settle down and write books.

I was the middle child of three, but there was a gap of five years on either side, and I barely saw my father before I was eight. For this and other reasons I was somewhat lonely, and I soon developed disagreeable mannerisms which made me unpopular throughout my schooldays. I had the lonely child's habit of making up stories and holding conversations with imaginary persons, and I think from the very start my literary ambitions were mixed up with the feeling of being isolated and undervalued. I knew that I had a facility with words and a power of facing unpleasant facts, and I felt that this created a sort of private world in which I could get my own back for my failure in everyday life. Nevertheless the volume of serious – i.e. seriously intended – writing which I produced all through my childhood and boyhood would not amount to half a dozen pages. I wrote my first poem at the age of four or five, my mother taking it down to dictation. I cannot remember anything about it except that it was about a tiger and the tiger had 'chair-like teeth' – a good enough phrase, but I fancy the poem was a plagiarism of Blake's 'Tiger, Tiger'. At eleven, when the war or 1914–18 broke out, I wrote a patriotic poem which was printed in the local newspaper, as was another, two years later, on the death of Kitchener. From time to time, when I was a bit older, I wrote bad and usually unfinished 'nature poems' in the Georgian style. I also attempted a short story which was a ghastly failure. That was the total of the would-be serious work that I actually set down on paper during all those years.

However, throughout this time I did in a sense engage in literary activities. To begin with there was the made-to-order stuff which I produced quickly, easily and without much pleasure to myself. Apart from school work, I wrote *vers d'occasion*, semi-comic poems which I could turn out at what now seems to me astonishing speed – at fourteen I wrote a whole rhyming play, in imitation of Aristophanes, in about a week – and helped to edit a school magazines, both printed and in manuscript. These magazines were the most pitiful burlesque stuff that you could imagine, and I took far less trouble with them than I now would with the cheapest journalism. But side by side with all this, for fifteen years or more, I was carrying out a literary exercise of a quite different kind: this was the making up of a continuous 'story' about myself, a sort of diary existing only in the mind. I believe this is a common habit of children and adolescents. As a very small child I used to imagine that I was, say, Robin Hood, and picture myself as the hero of thrilling adventures, but quite soon my 'story' ceased to be narcissistic in a crude way and became more and more a mere description of what I was doing and the things I saw. For minutes at a time this kind of thing would be running through my head: 'He pushed the door open and entered the room. A yellow beam of sunlight, filtering through the muslin curtains, slanted on to the table, where a match-box, half-open, lay beside the inkpot. With his right hand in his pocket he moved across to the window. Down in the street a tortoiseshell cat was chasing a dead leaf', etc. etc. This habit continued until I was about twenty-five, right through my non-literary years. Although I had to search, and did search, for the right words, I seemed to be making this descriptive effort almost against my will, under a kind of compulsion from outside. The 'story' must, I suppose, have reflected the styles of the various writers I admired at different ages, but so far as I remember it always had the same meticulous descriptive quality.

When I was about sixteen I suddenly discovered the joy
of mere words, i.e. the sounds and associations of words.
The lines from *Paradise Lost* –

> So hee with difficulty and labour hard
> Moved on: with difficulty and labour hee.

which do not now seem to me so very wonderful, sent
shivers down my backbone; and the spelling 'hee' for 'he' was
an added pleasure. As for the need to describe things, I knew
all about it already. So it is clear what kind of books I wanted
to write, in so far as I could be said to want to write books at
that time. I wanted to write enormous naturalistic novels with
unhappy endings, full of detailed descriptions and arresting
similes, and also full of purple passages in which words were
used partly for the sake of their own sound. And in fact my first
completed novel, *Burmese Days*, which I wrote when I was thirty
but projected much earlier, is rather that kind of book.

I give all this background information because I do not
think one can assess a writer's motives without knowing
something of his early development. His subject matter will
be determined by the age he lives in – at least this is true in
tumultuous, revolutionary ages like our own – but before
he ever begins to write he will have acquired an emotional
attitude from which he will never completely escape. It is his
job, no doubt, to discipline his temperament and avoid getting
stuck at some immature stage, in some perverse mood; but if
he escapes from his early influences altogether, he will have
killed his impulse to write. Putting aside the need to earn a
living, I think there are four great motives for writing, at any
rate for writing prose. They exist in different degrees in every
writer, and in any one writer the proportions will vary from
time to time, according to the atmosphere in which he
is living. They are:

(i) *Sheer egoism.* Desire to seem clever, to be talked about, to be remembered after death, to get your own back on the grown-ups who snubbed you in childhood, etc., etc. It is humbug to pretend this is not a motive, and a strong one. Writers share this characteristic with scientists, artists, politicians, lawyers, soldiers, successful businessmen – in short, with the whole top crust of humanity. The great mass of human beings are not acutely selfish. After the age of about thirty they almost abandon the sense of being individuals at all – and live chiefly for others, or are simply smothered under drudgery. But there is also the minority of gifted, willful people who are determined to live their own lives to the end, and writers belong in this class. Serious writers, I should say, are on the whole more vain and self-centered than journalists, though less interested in money.

(ii) *Aesthetic enthusiasm.* Perception of beauty in the external world, or, on the other hand, in words and their right arrangement. Pleasure in the impact of one sound on another, in the firmness of good prose or the rhythm of a good story. Desire to share an experience which one feels is valuable and ought not to be missed. The aesthetic motive is very feeble in a lot of writers, but even a pamphleteer or writer of textbooks will have pet words and phrases which appeal to him for non-utilitarian reasons; or he may feel strongly about typography, width of margins, etc. Above the level of a railway guide, no book is quite free from aesthetic considerations.

(iii) *Historical impulse.* Desire to see things as they are, to find out true facts and store them up for the use of posterity.

(iv) *Political purpose.* – Using the word 'political' in the widest possible sense. Desire to push the world in a certain direction, to alter other peoples' idea of the kind of society that they should strive after. Once again, no book is genuinely free from political bias. The opinion that art should have nothing to do with politics is itself a political attitude.

Being a writer means taking the leap
from listening to saying, 'Listen to me.'
Jhumpa Lahiri

Ian McEwan   Writers read each other obviously;
they are bound to deny it, but they
write for each other too, in a remote
and buried sense. This is particularly
true for those at the beginning of
their careers. We might prefer to
portray ourselves as lonely beacons in
a dark world, but when our first stories
or poems are printed it means a lot to
know that a few contemporaries we
admire are reading them.

Mary Shelley

It is not singular that, as the daughter of two persons of distinguished literary celebrity, I should very early in life have thought of writing. As a child I scribbled; and my favourite pastime, during the hours given me for recreation, was to 'write stories'. Still I had a dearer pleasure than this, which was the formation of castles in the air – the indulging in waking dreams – the following up trains of thought, which had for their subject the formation of a succession of imaginary incidents. My dreams were at once more fantastic and agreeable than my writings. In the latter I was a close imitator – rather doing as others had done, than putting down the suggestions of my own mind. What I wrote was intended at least for one other eye – my childhood's companion and friend; but my dreams were all my own; I accounted for them to nobody; they were my refuge when annoyed – my dearest pleasure when free.

We write to taste life twice, in the moment and in retrospection.
Anaïs Nin

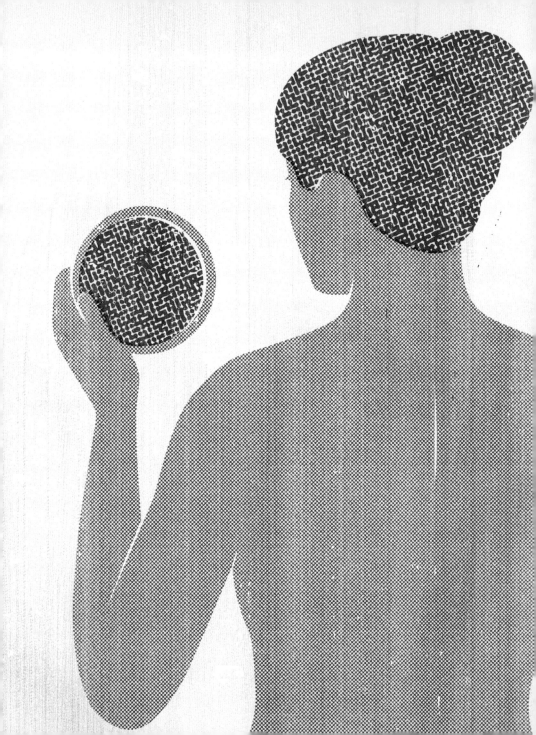

I was afraid to write because I was ashamed of my feelings and beliefs. The practice of any art can be a good excuse for self-loathing. You require a certain shamelessness to be any kind of artist. But to be shameless you need not to mind who you are.

Sometimes writers like to imagine that the difficulty of becoming a writer resides in convincing others that that is what you are. But really the problem is in convincing yourself.

Hanif Kureishi

F. Scott Fitzgerald

The history of my life is the history of the struggle between an overwhelming urge to write and a combination of circumstances bent on keeping me from it.

When I lived in St Paul and was about twelve I wrote all through every class in school in the back of my geography book and first year Latin and on the margins of themes and declensions and mathematics problems. Two years later a family congress decided that the only way to force me to study was to send me to boarding school. This was a mistake. It took my mind off my writing. I decided to play football, to smoke, to go to college, to do all sorts of irrelevant things that had nothing to do with the real business of life, which, of course, was the proper mixture of description and dialogue in the short story.

But in school I went off on a new tack. I saw a musical comedy called *The Quaker Girl*, and from that day forth my desk bulged with Gilbert & Sullivan librettos and dozens of notebooks containing the germs of dozens of musical comedies.

Near the end of my last year at school I came across a new musical-comedy score lying on top of the piano. It was a show called *His Honor the Sultan*, and the title furnished the information that it had been presented by the Triangle Club of Princeton University.

That was enough for me. From then on the university question was settled. I was bound for Princeton.

I spent my entire Freshman year writing an operetta for the

Triangle Club. To do this I failed in algebra, trigonometry, coordinate geometry and hygiene. But the Triangle Club accepted my show, and by tutoring all through a stuffy August I managed to come back a Sophomore and act in it as a chorus girl. A little after this came a hiatus. My health broke down and I left college one December to spend the rest of the year recuperating in the West. Almost my final memory before I left was of writing a last lyric on that year's Triangle production while in bed in the infirmary with a high fever.

The next year, 1916–17, found me back in college, but by this time I had decided that poetry was the only thing worth while, so with my head ringing with the meters of Swinburne and the matters of Rupert Brooke I spent the spring doing sonnets, ballads and rondels into the small hours. I had read somewhere that every great poet had written great poetry before he was twenty-one. I had only a year and, besides, war was impending. I must publish a book of startling verse before I was engulfed.

By autumn I was in an infantry officers' training camp at Fort Leavenworth, with poetry in the discard and a brand-new ambition – I was writing an immortal novel. Every evening, concealing my pad behind *Small Problems for Infantry*, I wrote paragraph after paragraph on a somewhat edited history of me and my imagination. The outline of twenty-two chapters, four of them in verse, was made, two chapters were completed; and then I was detected and the game was up. I could write no more during study period.

This was a distinct complication. I had only three months to live – in those days all infantry officers thought they had only three months to live – and I had left no mark on the world. But such consuming ambition was not to be thwarted by a mere war. Every Saturday at one o'clock when the week's work was over I hurried to the Officers' Club, and there, in a corner of a roomful of smoke, conversation and rattling newspapers, I wrote a one-hundred-and-twenty-thousand-word novel on the consecutive week-ends of three months. There was no revising; there was no time for it. As I finished each chapter I sent it to a typist in Princeton.

Meanwhile I lived in its smeary pencil pages. The drills, marches and *Small Problems for Infantry* were a shadowy dream. My whole heart was concentrated upon my book.

I went to my regiment happy. I had written a novel. The war could now go on. I forgot paragraphs and pentameters, similes and syllogisms. I got to be a first lieutenant, got my orders overseas – and then the publishers wrote me that though *The Romantic Egotist* was the most original manuscript they had received for years they couldn't publish it. It was crude and reached no conclusion.

It was six months after this that I arrived in New York and presented my card to the office boys of seven city editors asking to be taken on as a reporter. I had just turned twenty-two, the war was over, and I was going to trail murderers by day and do short stories by night. But the newspapers didn't need me. They sent their office boys out to tell me they didn't need me. They decided definitely and irrevocably by the sound of my name on a calling card that I was absolutely unfitted to be a reporter.

Instead I became an advertising man at ninety dollars a month, writing the slogans that while away the weary hours in rural trolley cars. After hours I wrote stories – from March to June. There were nineteen altogether; the quickest written in an hour and a half, the slowest in three days. No one bought them, no one sent personal letters. I had one hundred and twenty-two rejection slips pinned in a frieze about my room. I wrote movies. I wrote song lyrics. I wrote complicated advertising schemes. I wrote poems. I wrote sketches. I wrote jokes. Near the end of June I sold one story for thirty dollars.

On the Fourth of July, utterly disgusted with myself and all the editors, I went home to St Paul and informed family and friends that I had given up my position and had come home to write a novel. They nodded politely, changed the subject and spoke of me very gently. But this time I knew what I was doing. I had a novel to write at last, and all through two hot months I wrote and revised and compiled and boiled down. On September fifteen *This Side of Paradise* was accepted by special delivery.

In the next two months I wrote eight stories and sold nine. The ninth was accepted by the same magazine that had rejected it four months before. Then, in November, I sold my first story to the editors of *The Saturday Evening Post*. By February I had sold them half a dozen. Then my novel came out. Then I got married. Now I spend my time wondering how it all happened.

In the words of the immortal Julius Caesar: 'That's all there is; there isn't any more.'

I suppose one has to be desperate, to be a successful writer. One has to reach rock-bottom at which one can afford to let everything go hang. One has got to damn the public, chance one's living, say what one thinks, and be oneself. Then something may come out.
T.H. White

A writer is someone for whom writing is more difficult than it is for other people.
Thomas Mann

Jean Rhys

When I was excited about life, I didn't want to write at all. I've never written when I was happy. I didn't want to. But I've never had a long period of being happy. Do you think anyone has? I think you can be peaceful for a long time. When I think about it, if I had to choose, I'd rather be happy than write. You see there's very little invention in my books. What came first with most of them was the wish to get rid of this awful sadness that weighed me down. I found when I was a child that if I could put the hurt into words, it would go. It leaves a sort of melancholy behind and then it goes. I think it was Somerset Maugham who said that if you 'write out' a thing . . . it doesn't trouble you so much. You may be left with a vague melancholy, but at least it's not misery – I suppose it's like a Catholic going to confession, or like psychoanalysis.

Margaret Atwood

No writer emerges from childhood into a pristine environment, free from other people's biases about writers. All of us bump against a number of preconceptions about what we ought to be like, what constitutes good writing, and what social functions writing fulfils, or ought to fulfil. All of us develop our own ideas about what we are writing in relation to these preconceptions. Whether we attempt to live up to them, rebel against them, or find others using them to judge us, they affect our lives as writers . . .

. . . most people secretly believe they themselves have a book in them, which they would write if they could only find the time. And there's some truth to this notion. A lot of people do have a book in them – that is they have had an experience that other people might want to read about. But this is not the same thing as 'being a writer'.

Or, to put it in a more sinister way: everyone can dig a hole in a cemetery, but not everyone is a grave-digger. The latter takes a good deal more stamina and persistence. It is also, because of the nature of activity, a deeply symbolic role. As a grave-digger, you are not just a person who excavates. You carry upon your shoulders the weight of other people's projections, of their fears and fantasies and anxieties and superstitions. You represent mortality, whether you like it or not. And so it is with any public role, including that of the Writer, capital W; but also as with any public role, the significance of that role – its emotional and symbolic content – varies over time.

I know nothing in the world that has as much power as a word. Sometimes I write one, and I look at it, until it begins to shine.
Emily Dickinson

Among the numerous requisites that must concur to complete an author, few are of more importance than an early entrance into the living world. The seed of knowledge may be planted in solitude, but must be cultivated in public. Argumentation may be taught in colleges, and theories formed in retirement; but the artifice of embellishment and the powers of attraction can be gained only by a general converse.

Samuel Johnson

One night a friend lent me a book of short stories by Franz Kafka. I went back to the pension where I was staying and began to read 'The Metamorphosis'. The first line almost knocked me off the bed. I was so surprised. The first line reads, 'As Gregor Samsa awoke that morning from uneasy dreams, he found himself transformed in his bed into a gigantic insect . . .' When I read the line I thought to myself that I didn't know anyone was allowed to write things like that. If I had known, I would have started writing a long time ago. So I immediately started writing short stories.

Gabriel García Márquez

The writer has a grudge against society, which he documents with accounts of unsatisfying sex, unrealized ambition, unmitigated loneliness, and a sense of local and global distress.
Renata Adler

By the time I was fourteen (and shaving twice a week whether I needed to or not), the nail in my wall would no longer support the weight of the rejection slips impaled upon it. I replaced the nail with a spike and went on writing. By the time I was sixteen I'd begun to get rejection slips with hand-written notes a little more encouraging than the advice to stop using staples and start using paperclips. The first of these hopeful notes was from Algis Budrys, then the editor of *Fantasy and Science Fiction*, who read a story of mine called 'The Night of the Tiger' . . . and wrote: 'This is good. Not for us, but good. You have talent. Submit again.' Those four brief sentences, scribbled by a fountain pen that left big ragged blotches in its wake, brightened the dismal winter of my 16th year.
Stephen King

I am very grateful that I did start my career writing short stories because you really learn your craft. You can also learn to explore yourself; if you write a huge number of short stories it doesn't take you long to realise you have certain strengths and weaknesses and that your imagination leans toward one corner of the compass. I think young writers are tempted into writing novels far too early.

J.G. Ballard

When I was six I thought I was a writer. In some ways it has to do with the fact that I grew up in Nigeria. In Nigeria you become a doctor. We value engineers or doctors or lawyers. Writer? Hmm. It was always Why? Why would you want to become a writer? Sometimes when my American friends talk about finding it difficult to define themselves as writers, they assume that there's something presumptuous about saying 'I'm a writer.' For me, because of where I came from, I didn't have that. I just said 'Oh, I like to tell stories, I like to write them down.' If anything, what I made the conscious decision about was to try and be published. It's a really difficult thing. I had been writing forever, and if I hadn't been published I would still be writing, but the choice I made was that I wanted to be published. I was fifteen, and I had a poem in a magazine in Nigeria. It was a huge deal for me. So maybe that's when I decided that I wanted to be published, because that's a decision that one has to make. It's something you pursue. It's a matter of physically sending things out.

Chimamanda Ngozi Adichie

Since I was seven I had wanted to be a painter, and my family had accepted this. They all thought that I would be a famous painter. But then something happened in my head – I realized that a screw was loose – and I stopped painting and immediately began writing my first novel.
Orhan Pamuk

If you spend enough time reading or writing, you find a voice, but you also find certain tastes. You find certain writers who when they write, it makes your own brain voice like a tuning fork, and you just resonate with them. And when that happens, reading those writers . . . becomes a source of unbelievable joy. It's like eating candy for the soul. And I sometimes have a hard time understanding how people who don't have that in their lives get through the day.
David Foster Wallace

David Mitchell

I was in my mid-twenties and daydreamed of being a writer. I wanted to do to other people what my favorite authors had done to me. I found myself in Japan teaching English, and had no idea what I was going to do with the rest of my life. I was very naïve. It was in back of my head: *You'll probably be a writer.*

I sent an appalling novel, the first three chapters and the plot synopsis – this is pre-Internet of course, it cost a fortune – to fifteen agents and five publishers in London. I got four responses. One of the agents sent a note back, 'This perhaps isn't the thing, but let me see the next thing you write.' That was very encouraging.

I took half a year off work and went on the Trans Siberian Railway. I filled up notebooks. These random thoughts began to coagulate into stories. Stories are great but nobody buys them. I thought, how can I turn these things into a novel? Well, sometimes a theme can be your glue. I looked at the stories and began to notice they were all answers to the question: Why do things happen? What if one thing happens in one story that makes the next story possible? This is life, this is reality. The infinity of tiny coincidences. Plot connections. I realized that was strong enough glue. I showed five of these to the man in London who'd earlier showed polite, cautious interest in my work and he said, 'You might have something here, my boy.' One night, a fax came in and I still remember it. It was a very cheap two-book deal with the publishers I'm still with, and that was one of the best days of my life. In the morning, I was afraid it was a dream. But there was the fax on the table and it was one of those gilded mornings where the world is fantastic.

Here is advice. Send the thing out and forget it. Quickly get to work on the next thing. Don't sit by the phone or watch your email. Don't hope. You've done a big thing by finishing something. Spend all the energy on possible despair. Avert that possible despair. Transfer the despair to the next manuscript. Right away, like the next day.

In retrospect, I would say that I turned into a writer when I played among the ruins left by the war in the heart of Berlin; when the streets in which I grew up became a giant construction site; when my mother allowed me to cut school to go ice-skating; when my father took me to excavations of walled fortresses; when I went dancing; when I fell in love; when I had my hair cut; when my neighbors had too much to drink; when one of my grandmothers told me about the camps in Siberia, and the other one about migrating; when I mixed bookbinders' glue; when I read whenever I had time. After I finished my studies, I became an opera director and a baker's assistant. That's when I decided to write my first long text, out of which came my first book.

Jenny Erpenbeck

People say, 'What advice do you have for people who want to be writers?' I say, they don't really need advice, they know they want to be writers, and they're gonna do it. Those people who know that they really want to do this and are cut out for it, they know it.
R.L. Stine

The most helpful quality a writer can cultivate is self-confidence – arrogance, if you can manage it. You write to impose yourself on the world, and you have to believe in your own ability when the world shows no sign of agreeing with you. A book isn't quickly achieved and the road to publication can be strewn with obstacles. It is especially important to be self-confident if you have no contacts and do not know other writers. If you are unpublished you can still say to yourself, 'I am a writer.' You should define yourself as such.

Hilary Mantel

J.K. Rowling

It was 1990. My then boyfriend and I had decided to move up to Manchester together. After a weekend's flat-hunting, I was travelling back to London on my own on a crowded train, and the idea for Harry Potter simply fell into my head.

I had been writing almost continuously since the age of six but I had never been so excited about an idea before. To my immense frustration, I didn't have a pen that worked, and I was too shy to ask anybody if I could borrow one . . .

I did not have a functioning pen with me, but I do think that this was probably a good thing. I simply sat and thought, for four (delayed train) hours, while all the details bubbled up in my brain, and this scrawny, black-haired, bespectacled boy who didn't know he was a wizard became more and more real to me.

Perhaps, if I had slowed down the ideas to capture them on paper, I might have stifled some of them (although sometimes I do wonder, idly, how much of what I imagined on that journey I had forgotten by the time I actually got my hands on a pen). I began to write 'Philosopher's Stone' that very evening, although those first few pages bear no resemblance to anything in the finished book.

Haruki Murakami

I can pinpoint the exact moment when I first thought I could write a novel. It was around one thirty in the afternoon of April 1, 1978. I was at Jingu Stadium that day, alone in the outfield drinking beer and watching the game. Jingu Stadium was within walking distance of my apartment at the time, and I was a fairly big Yakult Swallows fan. It was a perfectly beautiful spring day, not a cloud in the sky, with a warm breeze blowing. There weren't any benches in the outfield seating back then, just a grassy slope. I was lying on the grass, sipping cold beer, gazing up occasionally at the sky, and leisurely enjoying the game. As usual for the Swallows, the stadium wasn't very crowded. It was the season opener, and they were taking on the Hiroshima Carp at home. I remember that Yasuda was pitching for the Swallows. He was a short, stocky sort of pitcher with a wicked curve. He easily retired the side in the top of the first inning, and in the bottom of the inning the leadoff batter for the Swallows was Dave Hilton, a young American player new to the team. Hilton got a hit down the left field line. The crack of bat meeting ball right on the sweet spot echoed through the stadium. Hilton easily rounded first and pulled up to second. And it was at that exact moment that a thought struck me: *You know what? I could try writing a novel.* I still can remember the wide open sky, the feel of the new grass, the satisfying crack of the bat. Something flew down from the sky at that instant, and whatever it was, I accepted it.

A great book may be an accident, but a good one is a possibility and it is thinking of that that one writes. In short, to achieve. The rest takes care of itself, and so much praise is given to insignificant things that there is hardly any sense in striving for it.

In the end writing is like a prison, an island from which you will never be released but which is a kind of paradise: the solitude, the thoughts, the incredible joy of putting into words the essence of what you for the moment understand and with your whole heart want to believe.

James Salter

First, try to be something, anything, else. A movie star/ astronaut. A movie star/missionary. A movie star/ kindergarten teacher. President of the World. Fail miserably. It is best if you fail at an early age – say, 14. Early, critical disillusionment is necessary so that at 15 you can write long haiku sequences about thwarted desire. It is a pond, a cherry blossom, a wind brushing against sparrow wing leaving for mountain. Count the syllables. Show it to your mom. She is tough and practical. She has a son in Vietnam and a husband who may be having an affair. She believes in wearing brown because it hides spots. She'll look briefly at your writing then back up at you with a face blank as a doughnut. She'll say: 'How about emptying the dishwasher?' Look away. Shove the forks in the fork drawer. Accidentally break one of the freebie gas station glasses. This is the required pain and suffering. This is only for starters.

Lorrie Moore

The way I felt when I was reading – that sense of a world created by words. I thought it would be fun to try that myself.

I do believe that there's such a thing as talent, but I think persistence is an even more important quality for a writer to possess. It can be a long road to get where you're going.
Tom Perrotta

We hear a lot about slanting for the commercial market, but not enough about slanting for the literary cliques, Both approaches, in the final analysis, are unhappy for a writer. No one remembers, no one brings up, no one discusses the slanted story, be in diminuendoed Hemingway or third-time-around Elinor Glyn.

What is the greatest reward a writer can have? Isn't it that way when someone rushes up to you, his face bursting with honesty, his eyes afire with admiration and cries, 'That new story of yours was fine, really wonderful!'

Then and only then is writing worthwhile.

Quite suddenly the pomposities of the intellectual faddists fade to dust. Suddenly, the agreeable monies collected from the fat-advertising magazines are unimportant.

The most callous of commercial writers loves that moment.

The most artificial of literary writers lives for that moment.
Ray Bradbury

When I was fifteen I wore a black straw hat with square holes punched in the brim and wrote on paper napkins in the greasy spoon by the bus station. I had a vague idea this was how writers were supposed to behave because I had read books about poets and philosophers drinking espresso in French cafés while they wrote about how unhappy they were. There were not many cafés like that in the UK at the time and certainly not in West Finchley. . . . I wrote . . . sentences very fast on the white paper napkins. This action (scribbling) and also my costume (the black hat) were like being armed with an AK-47: the sort of rifle the newspapers always showed third-world children holding instead of an ice cream with a flake bar stuck in the middle of it. As far as the builders sitting next to me were concerned, I was not quite there. I had written myself into some other kind of status and they didn't feel easy about chatting me up or asking me to pass the salt. I was out if it.

Writing made me feel wiser than I actually was. Wise and sad. That was what I thought writers should be.

Deborah Levy

It's easy, after all, not to be a writer. Most people aren't writers, and very little harm comes to them.

Julian Barnes

METHODS AND MEANS

Getting down to it

Anthony Trollope

It was my practice to be at my table every morning at 5.30 A.M.; and it was also my practice to allow myself no mercy. An old groom, whose business it was to call me, and to whom I paid £5 a year extra for the duty, allowed himself no mercy. During all those years at Waltham Cross he was never once late with the coffee which it was his duty to bring me. I do not know that I ought not to feel that I owe more to him than to any one else for the success I have had. By beginning at that hour I could complete my literary work before I dressed for breakfast.

All those I think who have lived as literary men – working daily as literary labourers – will agree with me that three hours a day will produce as much as a man ought to write. But then he should so have trained himself that he shall be able to work continuously during those three hours – so have tutored his mind that it shall not be necessary for him to sit nibbling his pen, and gazing at the wall before him, till he shall have found the words with which he wants to express his ideas.

It had at this time become my custom – and it still is my custom, though of late I have become a little lenient to myself – to write with my watch before me, and to require from myself 250 words every quarter of an hour. I have found that the 250 words have been forthcoming as regularly as my watch went. But my three hours were not devoted entirely to writing. I always began my task by reading the work of the day before, an operation which would take me half an hour, and which consisted chiefly in weighing with my ear the sound of the words and phrases. I would strongly recommend this practice to all tyros in writing.

That their work should be read after it has been written is a matter of course – that it should be read twice at least before it goes to the printers, I take to be a matter of course. But by reading what he has last written, just before he recommences his task, the writer will catch the tone and spirit of what he is then saying, and will avoid the fault of seeming to be unlike himself. This division of time allowed me to produce over ten pages of an ordinary novel volume a day, and if kept up through ten months, would have given as its results three novels of three volumes each in the year.

I always write in the morning. I was pleased to hear lately that Rousseau too, after he got up in the morning, went for a short walk and sat down to work. In the morning one's head is particularly fresh. The best thoughts most often come in the morning after waking, while still in bed or during the walk. Many writers work at night. Dostoevsky always wrote at night. In a writer there must always be two people – the writer and the critic. And, if one works at night, with a cigarette in one's mouth, although the work of creation goes on briskly, the critic is for the most part in abeyance, and this is very dangerous.

Leo Tolstoy

I can say I have never found alcohol helpful to literary production in any degree. My experience goes to prove that the effect of wine, taken as a preliminary to imaginative work, as it is called, is to blind the writer to the quality of what he produced rather than to raise its quality.

Thomas Hardy

Walter Scott

But, to confess to you the truth, the works and passages in which I have succeeded, have uniformly been written with the greatest rapidity; and when I have seen some of these placed in opposition with others, and commended as more highly finished, I could appeal to pen and standish, that the parts in which I have come feebly off, were by much the more laboured. Besides, I doubt the beneficial effect of too much delay, both on account of the author and the public. A man should strike while the iron is hot, and hoist sail while the wind is fair. If a successful author keep not the stage, another instantly takes his ground. If a writer lie by for ten years ere he produces a second work, he is superseded by others; or, if the age is so poor of genius that this does not happen, his own reputation becomes his greatest obstacle. The public will expect the new work to be ten times better than its predecessor; the author will expect it should be ten times more popular, and 'tis a hundred to ten that both are disappointed. . . .

I will venture to say, that no work of imagination, proceeding from the mere consideration of a certain sum of copy-money, ever did, or ever will, succeed. So the lawyer who pleads, the soldier who fights, the physician who prescribes, the clergyman – if such there be – who preaches, without any zeal for his profession, or without any sense of its dignity, and merely on account of the fee, pay, or stipend, degrade themselves to the rank of sordid mechanics. Accordingly, in the case of two of the learned faculties at least, their services are considered as unappreciable, and are acknowledged, not by any exact estimate of the services rendered, but by a *honorarium*, or voluntary acknowledgment. But let a client or patient make the experiment of omitting this little ceremony of the *honorarium*, which is *censé* to be a thing entirely out of consideration between them, and mark how the learned gentleman will look upon his case. Cant set apart, it is the same thing with literary emolument. No man of sense, in any rank of life, is, or ought to be, above accepting a just recompense for his time, and a reasonable share of the capital which owes its very existence to his exertions. When Czar Peter wrought in the trenches, he took the pay of a common soldier; and nobles, statesmen, and divines, the most distinguished of their time, have not scorned to square accounts with their bookseller . . . no man of honour, genius, or spirit, would make the mere love of gain, the chief, far less the only, purpose of his labours. For myself, I am not displeased to find the game a winning one; yet while I pleased the public, I should probably continue it merely for the pleasure of playing; for I have felt as strongly as most folks that love of composition, which is perhaps the strongest of all instincts, driving the author to the pen, the painter to the pallet, often without either the chance of fame or the prospect of reward. Perhaps I have said too much of this. I might, perhaps, with as much truth as most people, exculpate myself from the charge of being either of a greedy or mercenary disposition; but I am not, therefore, hypocrite enough to disclaim the ordinary motives, on account of which the whole world around me is toiling unremittingly, to the sacrifice of ease, comfort, health, and life. I do not affect the disinterestedness of that ingenious association of gentlemen mentioned by Goldsmith, who sold their magazine for sixpence a-piece, merely for their own amusement.

Write while the heat is in you. When the farmer burns a hole in his yoke he carries the hot iron quickly from the fire to the wood for every moment it is less effectual to penetrate (pierce) it. It must be used instantly or it is useless. The writer who postpones the recording of his thoughts uses an iron which has cooled to burn a hole with. He cannot inflame the minds of his audience.

Henry David Thoreau

Kate Chopin   Eight or nine years ago I began to write stories – short stories which appeared in the magazines, and I forthwith began to suspect I had the writing habit. The public shared this impression, and called me an author. Since then, though I have written many short stories and a novel or two, I am forced to admit that I have not the writing habit. But it is hard to make people with the questioning habit believe this.

'How, where, when, why, what do you write?' are some of the questions that I remember. How do I write? On a lapboard with a block of paper, a stub pen, and a bottle of ink bought at the corner grocery, which keeps the best in town.

Where do I write? In a Morris chair beside the window, where I can see a few trees and a patch of sky, more or less blue.

When do I write? I am greatly tempted here to use slang and reply 'any old time', but that would lend a tone of levity to this bit of confidence, whose seriousness I want to keep intact if possible. So I shall say I write in the morning, when not too strongly drawn to struggle with the intricacies of a pattern, and in the afternoon, if the temptation to try a new furniture polish on an old table leg is not too powerful to be denied; sometimes at night, though as I grow older I am more and more inclined to believe that night was made for sleep.

'Why do I write?' is a question which I have often asked myself and never very satisfactorily answered. Story-writing – at least with me – is the spontaneous expression of impressions gathered goodness knows where. To seek the source, the impulse of a story is like tearing a flower to pieces for wantonness.

What do I write? Well, not everything that comes into my head, but much of what I have written lies between the covers of my books.

When they were growing up, my kids knew that
they came first with me – which meant I would
schedule tours, when possible, around school
plays and softball games and ballroom competitions.
It also meant that I was continually interrupted.
After I wrote about eight books my husband became
a stay-at-home dad. He carpooled, drove to and
from school, attended skating practice, etc. so that
I could go on tour for months at a time without
batting an eye; or work through school pickup at
2:45 P.M. without breaking stride; or hie off on a
research expedition without thinking twice. My
husband's choice to stay home was an amazing
gift to me – a freedom and ability to write whenever
I liked. But for many years, I had to squeeze in my
work around child care schedules, and that made
me develop a very firm discipline. I write quickly,
but I also do not believe in writer's block, because
once I didn't have the luxury of believing it. When
you only have twenty minutes, you write – whether
it's garbage, or it's good . . . you just DO it, and you
fix it later.

Jodi Picoult

I seem to be doing an average of 2,000 words a day now . . .
Only 13,000 words to be done. But they are very much
on my mind, When I am not working here, I am walking
in the forest and worrying over the invention, 5 to 7 miles
a day. . . . I rise at 5.45 and go to bed at 9.30.
Arnold Bennett

Don't dash off a six-thousand-word story
before breakfast. Don't write too much.
Concentrate your sweat on one story, rather
than dissipate it over a dozen. Don't loaf
and invite inspiration; light out after it with
a club, and if you don't get it you will none
the less get something that looks remarkably
like it. Set yourself a 'stint', and see that you
do that 'stint' each day; you will have more
words to your credit at the end of the year.

Study the tricks of the writers who have
arrived. They have mastered the tools with
which you are cutting your fingers. They
are doing things, and their work bears the
internal evidence of how it is done. Don't
wait for some good Samaritan to tell you,
Jack London   but dig it out for yourself.

At night, when the objective world has slunk back into its cavern and left dreamers to their own, there come inspirations and capabilities impossible at any less magical and quiet hour. No one knows whether or not he is a writer unless he has tried writing at night.
H.P. Lovecraft

Looking back, I imagine I was always writing. Twaddle it was too. But better far write twaddle or anything, anything, than nothing at all.
Katherine Mansfield

When I was an aspiring writer in my mid-twenties, I had something shocking: a real job. I worked in a bookshop in Dublin and would rise every morning at about five A.M. in order to write before going to work. In the two decades since then, I've never shaken off that routine and while I don't get up quite so early these days, I'm usually at my desk by about 7:30. I'm at my most creative, my most optimistic and my most enthusiastic in the early mornings. I was fortunate enough to study under Malcolm Bradbury during his final year teaching the Creative Writing MA at the University of East Anglia and always remember his advice that we should write every day, 'even Christmas Day', and for the most part I stick with that. I'm not quite sure what to do with days off.

John Boyne

James Joyce

A book in my opinion should not be planned out beforehand, but as one writes it will form itself, subject, as I say, to the constant emotional promptings of one's personality.

Always stop while you are going good and don't worry about it until you start to write the next day. That way your subconscious will work on it all the time. But if you think about it consciously or worry about it you will kill it and your brain will be tired before you start. Once you are into the novel it is as cowardly to worry about whether you can go on the next day as to worry about having to go into inevitable action. You *have* to go on. So there no sense to worry. You have to learn that to write a novel. The hard part about a novel is to finish it.

Ernest Hemingway

I may – and quite frequently do – plan out every scene, sometimes even every conversation, in a novel before I sit down to write it. But unless I know the history back to the remotest times of any place of which I am going to write, I cannot begin the work. And I must know – from personal observation, not reading – the shapes of windows, the nature of doorknobs, the aspects of kitchens, the material of which dresses are made, the leather used in shoes, the method used in manuring fields, the nature of bus tickets. I shall never use any of these things in the book. But unless I know what sort of doorknob his fingers closed on, how shall I – satisfactorily to myself – get my character out of doors?

Ford Madox Ford

C.S. Lewis

We now settled into a routine which has ever since served in my mind as an archetype, so that what I still mean when I speak of a 'normal' day (and lament that normal days are so rare) is a day of the Bookham pattern. For if I could please myself I would always live as I lived there. I would choose always to breakfast at exactly eight and to be at my desk by nine, there to read or write till one. If a cup of good tea or coffee could be brought me about eleven, so much the better. A step or so out of doors for a pint of beer would not do quite so well; for a man does not want to drink alone and if you meet a friend in the taproom the break is likely to be extended beyond its ten minutes. At one precisely lunch should be on the table; and by two at the latest I would be on the road. Not, except at rare intervals, with a friend. Walking and talking are two very great pleasures, but it is a mistake to combine them. Our own noise blots out the sounds and silences of the outdoor world; and talking leads almost inevitably to smoking, and then farewell to nature as far as one of our senses is concerned. The only friend to walk with is one (such as I found, during the holidays, in Arthur) who so exactly shares your taste for each mood of the countryside that a glance, a halt, or at most a nudge, is enough to assure us that the pleasure is shared. The return from the walk, and the arrival of tea, should be exactly coincident, and not later than a quarter past four. Tea should be taken in solitude, as I took it as Bookham on those (happily numerous) occasions when Mrs Kirkpatrick was out; the Knock himself disdained this meal. For eating and reading are two pleasures that combine admirably. Of course not all books are suitable for mealtime reading. It would be a kind of blasphemy to read poetry at table. What one wants is a gossipy, formless book which can be opened anywhere. The ones I learned so to use at Bookham were Boswell, and a translation of Herodotus, and Lang's *History of English Literature. Tristram Shandy, Elia* and the *Anatomy of Melancholy* are all good for the same purpose. At five a man should be at work again, and at it till seven. Then, at the evening meal and after, comes the time for talk, or, failing that, for lighter reading; and unless you are making a night of it with your cronies (and at Bookham I had none) there is no reason why you should ever be in bed later than eleven. But when is a man to write his letters? You forget that I am describing the happy life I led with Kirk or the ideal life I would live now if I could. And it is essential of the happy life that a man would have almost no mail and never dread the postman's knock.

You can approach the act of writing with nervousness, excitement, hopefulness, or even despair – the sense that you can never completely put on the page what's in your mind and heart. You can come to the act with your fists clenched and your eyes narrowed, ready to kick ass and take down names. You can come to it because you want a girl to marry you or because you want to change the world. Come to it any way but lightly. Let me say it again: *you must not come lightly to the blank page.*
Stephen King

Planning to write is not writing. Outlining, researching, talking to people about what you're doing, none of that is writing. Writing is writing.
E.L. Doctorow

A novel can't be thought into existence, it has to be written. The hands are always wiser than the head. . . . The way my main characters often drift through life, apparently without aim – the way they allow themselves to be pulled along by events and suddenly find themselves standing on the wrong street corner or bedding down on some stranger's sofa quite without design – is reflective of the way I write them into being. To plan out a novel in any strong sense just wouldn't work for me. I need a good opening sentence, and preferably the closing one too, in order to get started

Helle Helle

There is one myth about writers that I have always felt as particularly pernicious and untruthful – the myth of the 'lonely writer', the myth that writing is a lonely occupation, involving much suffering because, supposedly, the writer exists in a state of sensitivity which cuts him off, or raises him above, or casts him below the community around him. This is a common cliché, a hangover probably from the romantic period and the idea of the artist as Sufferer and Rebel.

Probably any of the arts that are not performed in a chorus-line are going to come in for a certain amount of romanticizing, but it seems to me particularly bad to do this to writers and especially fiction writers, because fiction writers engage in the homeliest, and most concrete, and most unromanticizable of all arts. I suppose there have been enough genuinely lonely suffering novelists to make this seem a reasonable myth, but there is every reason that such cases are the result of less admirable qualities in these writers, qualities which have nothing to do with vocation of writing itself.

Unless the novelist has gone utterly out of his mind, his aim is still communication, and communication suggests talking inside a community.

Flannery O'Connor

Belief & technique for modern prose

1 .... Scribbled secret notebooks, and wild
typewritten pages, for yr own joy

2 .... Submissive to everything, open, listening

3 .... Try never get drunk outside yr own house

4 .... Be in love with yr life

5 .... Something that you feel will find its own form

6 .... Be crazy dumbsaint of the mind

7 .... Blow as deep as you want to blow

8 .... Write what you want bottomless from bottom
of the mind

9 .... The unspeakable visions of the individual

10 .... No time for poetry but exactly what is

11 .... Visionary tics shivering in the chest

12 .... In tranced fixation dreaming upon object
before you

13 .... Remove literary, grammatical and
syntactical inhibition

14 .... Like Proust be an old teahead of time

15 .... Telling the true story of the world in
interior monolog

16 .... The jewel center of interest is the eye
within the eye

17 .... Write in recollection and amazement
for yourself

18 .... Work from pithy middle eye out, swimming
in language sea

19 .... Accept loss forever

20 .... Believe in the holy contour of life

21 .... Struggle to sketch the flow that already exists
intact in mind

22 .... Dont think of words when you stop but to
see picture better

23 .... Keep track of every day the date emblazoned
in yr morning

24 .... No fear or shame in the dignity of yr experience,
language & knowledge

25 .... Write for the world to read and see yr exact
pictures of it

26 .... Bookmovie is the movie in words, the visual
American form

27 .... In praise of Character in the Bleak inhuman
Loneliness

28 .... Composing wild, undisciplined, pure,
coming in from under, crazier the better

29 .... You're a Genius all the time

30 .... Writer-Director of Earthly movies Sponsored
& Angeled in Heaven

Jack Kerouac

I write and re-write. If you want to get the effect, it seems to me that the first thing you have to do is to write the thing done as it comes into your mind – the slush – and so get one idea of the shape of it. In this preliminary process, no doubt, one can write a good many thousand words a day, perhaps seven or eight thousand. But when all that is finished, it will take seven or eight solid days to pick it to pieces again and knock it straight.

The 'slush' effort of 'The Invisible Man' came to more than 100,000 words; the final outcome of it amours to 55,000. My first tendency was to make it much shorter still.

I used feel a great deal ashamed of this method. I thought it simply showed incapacity, and inability to hit the right nail on the head. This process is like this:

1	....	Worry and confusion.
2	....	Testing the idea, and trying to settle the question. Is the idea any good?
3	....	Throwing the idea away; getting another; finally returning, perhaps to the first.
4	....	The next thing is possibly a bad start.
5	....	Grappling with the idea with the feeling it has to be done.
6	....	Then the slush work, which I've already described.
7	....	Reading this over, and taking out what you think is essential, and re-writing the essential part of it,
8	....	After is has been type-written, you cut it about, so it has to be re-typed.
9	....	The result of your labour finds its way into print, and you take hold of the first opportunity to go over the whole thing again.

H.G. Wells

When you're writing a book, it's rather like going on a very long walk, across valleys and mountains and things, and you get the first view of what you see and you write it down. Then you walk a bit further, maybe up onto the top of a hill, and you see something else. Then you write that and you go on like that, day after day, getting different views of the same landscape really. The highest mountain on the walk is obviously the end of the book, because it's got to be the best view of all, when everything comes together and you can look back and see that everything you've done all ties up. But it's a very, very long, slow process.

Roald Dahl

If you want to concentrate deeply on some problem, and especially some piece of writing or paper-work, you should acquire a cat. Alone with the cat in the room where you work, I explained, the cat will invariably get up on your desk and settle placidly under the desk lamp. The light from a lamp, I explained, gives a cat great satisfaction. The cat will settle down and be serene, with a serenity that passes all understanding. And the tranquility of the cat will gradually come to affect you, sitting there at your desk, so that all the excitable qualities that impede your concentration compose themselves and give your mind back the self-command it has lost. You need not watch the cat all the time. Its presence alone is enough. The effect of a cat on your concentration is remarkable, very mysterious.

Muriel Spark

On the eve of the first day I know what will happen in the first chapter. Then, day after day, chapter after chapter, I find what comes later. After I have started a novel I write a chapter each day, without ever missing a day. Because it is a strain, I have to keep pace with the novel. If, for example, I am ill for forty-eight hours, I have to throw away the previous chapters. And I never return to that novel.

Georges Simenon

What advice can an older writer presume to offer to a younger? Only what he or she might wish to have been told years ago. Don't be discouraged! Don't cast sidelong glances, and compare yourself to others among your peers! (Writing in not a race. No one really 'wins'. The satisfaction is in the effort, and rarely in the consequent rewards, if there are any.) And again, *write your heart out*.

Read widely, and without apology. Read what you want to read, not what someone tells you you should read. (As Hamlet remarks, 'I know not "should".') Immerse yourself in a writer you love, and read everything he or she has written, including the very earliest work. Especially the very earliest work. Before the great writer became great, or even good, he/she was groping for a way, fumbling to acquire a voice, perhaps just like you.

Write for your own time, if not for your own generation exclusively. You can't write for 'posterity' – it doesn't exist. You can't write for a departed world. You may be addressing, unconsciously, an audience that doesn't exist; you may he trying to please someone who won't be pleased, and who isn't worth pleasing.

Joyce Carol Oates

Fay Weldon

I began on a typewriter because I thought that's what other writers did – certainly Graham Greene does. Then I started to use a felt-tipped pen; it gives you a space between thought and language. It helps develop your style, gives space of adjectives, so you can amplify as you go along. Then you decide that if a thing is worth an adjective it's worth a sentence.

I write in the morning, when my head is clear and the coffee is relatively fresh . . . in a little room on the top floor of my house.

I started using fountain pens a few years ago, and appreciate the mess. It makes writing feel like a kind of physical labor.

I have to produce something new before I let myself quit for the day.
Tom Perrotta

I was a lot dumber when I was writing the novel. I felt like worse of a writer because I wrote many of the short stories in one sitting or over maybe three days, and they didn't change that much. There weren't many, many drafts. That made me feel semi-brilliant and part of a magical process. Writing the novel wasn't like that. I would come home every day from my office and say, 'Well, I still really like the story, I just wish it was better written.' At that point, I didn't realize I was writing a first draft. And the first draft was the hardest part. From there, it was comparatively easy. It was like I had some Play-Doh to work with and could just keep working with it – doing a million drafts and things changing radically and characters appearing and disappearing and solving mysteries: Why is this thing here? Should I just take that away? And then realizing, no, that is there, in fact, because that is the key to this. I love that sort of detective work, keeping the faith alive until all the questions have been sleuthed out.
Miranda July

Annie Dillard

I do not so much write a book as sit up with it, as a dying friend. During visiting hours, I enter its room with dread and sympathy for its many disorders. I hold its hand and hope it will get better.

This tender relationship can change in a twinkling. If you skip a visit or two, a work in progress will turn on you.

A work in progress quickly becomes feral. It reverts to a wild state overnight. It is barely domesticated, a mustang on which you one day fastened a halter, but which now you cannot catch. It is a lion you cage in your study. As the work grows, it gets harder to control; it is a lion growing in strength. You must visit it every day and reassert your master over it. If you skip a day, you are quite rightly, afraid to open the door to its room. You enter its room with bravura a chair at the thing and shouting, 'Simba!'

Isaac Asimov

Thinking is the activity I love best, and writing to me is simply thinking through my fingers. I can write up to 18 hours a day. Typing 90 words a minute. I've done better than 50 pages a day. Nothing interferes with my concentration. You could put on an orgy in my office and I wouldn't look up – well, maybe once.

Hanif Kureishi   One of the conditions of being a
writer is the ability to bear and enjoy
solitude. Sometimes you get up from
your desk under the impression that
your inner world had more meaning
that the Real one. Yet solitude – the
condition of all important creative and intellectual work –
isn't something we're taught, nor is it much attended to as a
necessary human practise. People often avoid the solitude
they need because they feel guilty at leaving other people out.
But communing with yourself, the putting aside of time for
the calm exploration of inner states where experience can be
processed, where dim intuitions, the unclear and inchoate
can be examined, and where the undistracted mind drifts
and considers what it requires, is essential. In this solitude
there may be helplessness. You may be aware of too much
experience, and an inability to see, for some time, what the
creative possibilities are.

The solitude of writing is not the same as loneliness or
isolation. When the words are flowing the self disappears and
your anxieties, doubts and reservations are suspended. There
isn't a self to be lonely. But such solitude can become mixed
up with loneliness. You can delude yourself that everything
you need can be obtained within, in the imagination; that
people you create and move around as characters can supply
everything that real people can. In a sense you are asking
too much of your art. You have to learn to separate these
things out. In that sense writing, or becoming a writer is, like
sexuality, a paradigm for all one's learning, and for all one's
relationships.

The laptop computer is teeny. I loathe computers more and more, so I have one I can shut down and shelve like a book. On the right of the desk is one of the two Olivetti Lettera 22s I own – beautiful machines. On top of it is the typescript of my next novel, *The Butt*. My books begin life in notebooks, then they move on to Post-it notes, the Post-its go up on the walls of the room. The shaggy patch of them in the middle of the wall (they're stuck to a map of the Isle of Grain, my spiritual home) are all short story ideas, tropes, metaphors, gags, characters, etc. When I'm working on a book, the Post-its come down off the wall and go into scrapbooks, which is why the wall to the left of the window has Post-it alopecia – that's where some of *The Book of Dave* was stuck up. I can't throw anything away. Anything. I'm going to end up like one of those old weirdos who lives in a network of tunnels burrowed through trash – yet I do not fear this.

Will Self

You get ideas from daydreaming. You get ideas from being bored. You get ideas all the time. The only difference between writers and other people is we notice when we're doing it.
Neil Gaiman

I have never written with an audience in mind, including me, nor can I conceive of my ability to do so. The words always present themselves of their own accord and as their own creature; or at least that's the subjective feeling. The matter is even more pronounced. I've learnt never to go looking, but to be patient. Arthur Koestler spoke once for all: 'Soak, and wait.'
Alan Garner

1 .... When still a child, make sure you read a lot of books. Spend more time doing this than anything else.

2 .... When an adult, try to read your own work as a stranger would read it, or even better, as an enemy would.

3 .... Don't romanticise your 'vocation'. You can either write good sentences or you can't. There is no 'writer's lifestyle'. All that matters is what you leave on the page.

4 .... Avoid your weaknesses. But do this without telling yourself that the things you can't do aren't worth doing. Don't mask self-doubt with contempt.

5 .... Leave a decent space of time between writing something and editing it.

6 .... Avoid cliques, gangs, groups. The presence of a crowd won't make your writing any better than it is.

7 .... Work on a computer that is disconnected from the Internet.

8 .... Protect the time and space in which you write. Keep everybody away from it, even the people who are most important to you.

9 .... Don't confuse honours with achievement.

10 .... Tell the truth through whichever veil comes to hand – but tell it. Resign yourself to the lifelong sadness that comes from never being satisfied.

Zadie Smith

Rivka Galchen

Everyone has their own eccentric habits that work best for them, some people do well to just hang around yabbering all day (or even for the first forty years of their life) and then stay up all night and work til dawn, and some people like to listen to music, and some people put cork on their walls to make life even more silent, and I guess Nabokov fussily wrote on those tiny notecards, and Trollope kept his job delivering the mail and so wrote just early in the morning but only took a ten minute break between novels, and managed to write more with his quill than anyone since with their superfast computers. Philip K. Dick, I believe on more than one occasion, got drugged up and wrote virtually nonstop without editing for 40 days and then had a brilliant novel at the end. (Whereas for most of us, such conditions probably wouldn't even generate a coherent email to mom.) So I guess people find their own way, and the only advice is to look seriously for it, even if looking for it might somehow mean not looking for it, etc.

For me though, I'm kind of a defender of maintaining a really boring life, of having the same habits every day; since life is inevitably kind of exhaustingly interesting if you pay the least bit of attention to it, it's not a bad idea to cordon off a part of it for reliability and repetition. Like: I know I write best in the morning, and the coffee shop in my neighborhood opens up at 7:30 and getting there around opening time kind of lends the structure to my writing day. I like to sit there, eat my two cookies with my tea, and feel my job is to write. For much of working on this novel, I only had until 10:30 am to myself, and then had to teach or attend to some other obligation, but that was still a lot of time. And it's great there – no internet, no music, the same-ish handful of morning regulars. I find it so, so comforting. And even if I think I have no ideas that day, I try not to luxuriate in that depressed feeling, and instead try to just write something bad, figuring it'll somehow help me write something better on another day. For me this kind of plodding regularity is the only thing that brings out the ghosts. And there's no good writing without the ghosts. (I feel like in order for me to like something I've written, I need to get to that place where it doesn't feel like it's me writing, but instead me transcribing, which sounds moronically antique – even to me – but, there you go, somehow it still seems right(ish).) But I feel like I can't just go about my life and wait for haunting. Instead – it's kind of like those people who keep a little shrine in some corner of their home. I saw a lot of this in various parts of South America. You've got this little shrine, and you tend to it in all these really prosaic ways: dust it, give it its daily incense, occasionally a sifter of brandy, a cigar, whatever seems likely to appeal to the spirit. And sometimes the shrine looks not haunted at all, but the space is there ready, for whenever the spirit comes. So, well, that's how I think of habits, that they're like tending to a little shrine of time.

Read, read, read. Read everything – trash, classics, good and bad, and see how they do it. Just like a carpenter who works as an apprentice and studies the master. Read! You'll absorb it. Then write. If it is good, you'll find out. If it's not, throw it out the window.

William Faulkner

The *writing* writing that I do is longhand. . . . The first two or three drafts are always longhand. . . . I can type very much faster than I can write. And writing makes me slow down in a way that helps me pay attention.

David Foster Wallace

The alarm clock would go off at 5, and I'd jump in the shower. My office was 5 minutes away. And I had to be at my desk, at my office, with the first cup of coffee, a legal pad and write the first word at 5:30, five days a week.

John Grisham

Each succeeding novel of mine has felt like the hardest to write. This partly has to do with my expectation that the work ought to become easier as I become more practised. But every time I try to start a novel I feel like I've never written one before – the whole process has to be rediscovered, reinvented. It's similar to tennis: there are days when I go out on the court and the racquet feels like some Neanderthal club that I've never touched in my life. I take a certain amount of pride in my inability to become a professional novelist. But it can be excruciating from day to day. . . . The task is always to develop a set of characters whom I can love enough to put them through torments which, without love, would simply be cruel. There seems to be no way to perform this task but through trial and error: lots of fragmentary beginnings; lots of notes which, almost as soon as I've written them, become so boring that I can't even read them. It's hideously frustrating, but I haven't figured out a faster way to work.

Rendering a world is a matter of permitting oneself to feel small things intensely, not of knowing lots of information. And so, when I'm working, I need to isolate myself at the office, because I'm easily distracted and modern life has become extremely distracting. Distraction pours through every portal, especially through the internet. And most of what pours through is meaningless noise. To be able to hear what's really happening in the world, you have to block out 99% of the noise. The remaining 1% is still a lot of information, but it's not so much that don't you have some hope of fashioning a meaningful narrative out of it.

Jonathan Franzen

Why use a pen or pencil when everything you put down will have to be typed up anyway? (That would be my answer right there: use a pen or pencil because what you put down will then have to be typed up.)

For many writers, of previous generations, the treble moment of transition from manuscript to typescript was one of great insight. Treble because there is first the moment of rereading the original words with a view to typing them up. I call this rereading but, in truth, it may be the first time these words are read rather than written.

As the eyes of the typer-upper, i.e., you, go over the notebook or A4 page, the reverse of the envelope or the inky palm, small decisions and revisions are being made – do I really type all of this? Are there words I've clearly misspelled or, in haste, chosen badly? Also, even before this, there is estrangement: here is your best chance of reading what you have written as if it had been written by someone else.

Secondly, there is the moment of typing itself, where the continuance of a sentence – the long keeping-going before the right ring-finger can hit the full-stop key and the thumb the space bar – begins to seem intolerable, or the number of times (I've only just noticed) that words in this paragraph begin with 's' or just that you've used 'what' and 'that' six times in four lines – that is another moment of self-scrutiny.

Thirdly, there is the turning of irregular pages into regular ones – the final glance as you scroll down and down, that tells you the scene goes on for five pages, and does it really need to go on for five pages, and that you haven't written any dialogue within living memory.

There's also a fourthly, perhaps, which is the moment of seeing the typescript as you print it out.

Plus, if you handwrite, you will write initially in anticipation of having to type up rather than type in the knowledge that you can, later on, always delete.

These are radically different working practices. If you're lazy, as most of us are, you won't want to retype unnecessary phrases or words. So, by virtue of being handwritten, your first draft is likely to be better already . . .

1 .... Marry somebody you love and who thinks
you being a writer's a good idea.

2 .... Don't have children.

3 .... Don't read your reviews.

4 .... Don't write reviews.
(Your judgment's always tainted.)

5 .... Don't have arguments with your wife in the
morning, or late at night.

6 .... Don't drink and write at the same time.

7 .... Don't write letters to the editor. (No one cares.)

8 .... Don't wish ill on your colleagues.

9 .... Try to think of others' good luck as
encouragement to yourself.

10 .... Don't take any shit if you can possibly help it.

Richard Ford

I had many years of stuffing large, unfinished manuscripts under my bed until finally I met the science-fiction writer Michael Moorcock who told me, 'You don't understand how to structure things. You have 160 pages divided into four parts, labelled "introduction of characters", "development of characters", and so on.' He wrote it all out for me with coloured pens and I'm eternally grateful, and always try to tell people that you have to become very humble and think: here are my 160 pages, I'm going to split it into parts, and then it's not so frightening. If you tell yourself, 'Here are my first ten pages, and in my first ten pages I must introduce, say, half my characters,' then you've already got something to do, introducing your characters in situations which show what they're like. This will then automatically lead you to think about the development of what's going to happen. Although this sounds so crass and crude, and as if it only belonged to a rather child-like science fiction, it can get a writer going, and away from that inchoate terror of a mountain of white paper. It's a general formula which makes you do it.

Emma Tennant

I have come to this resolution – never to write for the sake of writing or making a poem, but from running over with any little knowledge or experience which many years of reflection may perhaps give me; otherwise I shall be dumb.

John Keats

David Mitchell

We have a hard time remaining in the present: Our monkey minds are continually jumping through the jungles of the past and the forests of the future. . . .

The world is very good at distracting us. Much of the ingenuity of our remarkable species goes towards finding new ways to distract ourselves from things that really matter. The internet – it's lethal, isn't it? Maintaining focus is critical, I think, in the presence of endless distraction. You've only got time to be a halfway decent parent, plus one other thing.

For me, that one other thing is: I've got to be writing. I have a few ways to make sure I can carve out time.

Part one: Neglect everything else.

Part two: Get disciplined. Learn to rush to your laptop and open it up. Open the file without asking yourself if you're in the mood, without thinking about anything else. Just open the file: and then you're safe. Once the words are on the screen, that becomes your distraction.

Of course, it's not distraction – it's work, and it's wonderful when it goes well. I'm sure other, more disciplined people can do it without needing to rush, but I have to. The moment you think okay, it's work time, and face down the words, you rush past all the other things asking for your attention.

Part three: Keep the Apple homepage, because it's rather boring. If your homepage is the website of your favorite newspaper, you've had it.

Just remember, this is how you earn a living. Really hardworking people at the publisher's are relying on your next book for their bonuses, to feed their kids, pay their mortgage. You owe it to them not to let years fritter away fruitlessly.

First and foremost, of course, you owe it to yourself, and you owe it to your book – but if that isn't getting the job done, remember that it's other people's livelihoods on the line as well, not just yours.

These are just some of the sticks I use to beat myself into opening up the file. Once I do, I'm safe. I'm home free.

I do think there's some relationship between maintaining focus, looking closely, and the act of writing itself. The more you practice really looking, the more convincingly you can build a set for a scene. You become used to looking at the relationships between objects and people and light and time and mood and air. . . . I think all writers do this. I don't think I'm remarkably gifted at it or anything, but if there is an overlap between the skill of perception and the skill of populating a scene with objects and people, then this would be the connection.

Now that I'm forty-four years old, I'm going to offer
some advice on the art of writing short stories.

1 .... Never approach short stories one at a time.
If one approaches short stories one at a time, one
can quite honestly be writing the same short story
until the day one dies.

2 .... It is best to write short stories three or five at a
time. If one has the energy, write them nine or
fifteen at a time.

3 .... Be careful: the temptation to write short stories
two at a time is just as dangerous as attempting
to write them one at a time, and, what's more,
it's essentially like the interplay of lovers' mirrors,
creating a double image that produces melancholy.

4 .... One must read Horacio Quiroga, Felisberto
Hernández, and Jorge Luis Borges. One must
read Juan Rulfo and Augusto Monterroso. Any
short-story writer who has some appreciation for
these authors will never read Camilo José Cela
or Francisco Umbral yet will, indeed, read Julio
Cortázar and Adolfo Bioy Casares, but in no way
Cela or Umbral.

5 .... I'll repeat this once more in case it's still not clear:
don't consider Cela or Umbral, whatsoever.

6 .... A short-story writer should be brave. It's a sad fact
to acknowledge, but that's the way it is.

7 .... Short-story writers customarily brag about having
read Petrus Borel (Joseph-Pierre Borel). In fact,
many short-story writers are notorious for trying
to imitate Borel's writing. What a huge mistake!
Instead, they should imitate the way Borel dresses.

But the truth is that they hardly know anything about him – or Théophile Gautier or Gérard de Nerval!

8 .... Let's come to an agreement: read Petrus Borel, dress like Petrus Borel, but also read Jules Renard and Marcel Schwob. Above all, read Schwob, then move on to Alfonso Reyes and from there go to Borges.

9 .... The honest truth is that with Edgar Allan Poe, we would all have more than enough good material to read.

10 .... Give thought to point number 9. Think and reflect on it. You still have time. Think about number 9. To the extent possible, do so on bended knees.

11 .... One should also read a few other highly recommended books and authors – e.g., *Peri hypsous* (1st century A.D.; Eng. *On the Sublime*, 1554), by the notable Pseudo-Longinus; the sonnets of the unfortunate and brave Philip Sidney, whose biography Lord Brooke wrote; *The Spoon River Anthology* (1916), by Edgar Lee Masters; *Suicidios ejemplares* (1991; *Exemplary Suicides*), by Enrique Vila-Matas; and *Mientras ellas duermen* (1990; *While the Women Sleep*), by Javier Marías.

12 .... Read these books and also read Anton Chekhov and Raymond Carver, for one of the two of them is the best writer of the twentieth century.
Roberto Bolaño

Hilary Mantel

When you begin the work on a book mentally, before anything goes down on paper, you have a lot of ideas. You may find a location that seems of interest – or a name might pop into your head – or a phrase. It's important to capture these insights. I carry small notebooks, which I can easily tear pages from: or I carry 3 × 5 inch index cards. I try to put down every insight, every glimpse of what this book will be, even if it is only a word.

When I have a few of these cards I pin them up on a cork – notice board in the room where I work. You do not know at this stage what is important – that will emerge. You do not know the order of events – but you don't need to know. Ideas build around these glimpses, these key phrases. Perhaps I write something else on one of my cards, just a few words; or perhaps the original idea begins to develop, and I am moved to write a paragraph or two. I pin that paragraph behind the card to which it relates.

The little words breed – sometimes several hundreds of offspring. I keep them on the board, in any order, until one day I see a sequence, a logic, begin to emerge. Then I repin them, very approximately, very roughly, in the order in which I feel the narrative will take shape. A few weeks on, all these bits of paper – the original cards, and anything that has accumulated behind them – go into a ring binder. With a ring binder, you can easily swap pages around – you are still not committing yourself to an order of events. You can add pages, transpose pages. But, now you can begin to see how much of your book you have written. Some incidents, behind their original card, will be fully described, and some characters will come complete with their biographies, snatches of dialogue, their appearance and their way of talking.

I am amazed at how easily ideas fall into place, how they multiply, if you give them a chance and if you don't close off their possibilities too early. This is really a method of growing a book, rather than writing one.

The notion that one can write better during one season of the year than another Samuel Johnson labeled, 'Imagination operating on luxury.' Another luxury for an idle imagination is the writer's own feeling about the work. There is neither a proportional relationship, nor an inverse one, between a writer's estimation of a work in progress and its actual quality. The feeling that the work is magnificent, and the feeling that it is abominable, are both mosquitos to be repelled, ignored, or killed, but not indulged.

Annie Dillard

All through my career I've written 1,000 words a day – even if I've got a hangover. You've got to discipline yourself if you're professional. There's no other way.
J.G. Ballard

What do other people do? How do they write? Is there an easier way? No. I'm sorry, but there is no magic trick. You've just got to put your butt in the seat.

I have a small apartment in Manhattan, New York, with a desk in my bedroom, and that's the best spot for writing. I think for New York it's probably a good size apartment, and I've been working there for so long that I'm used to it. I've been there almost 25 years, which is too long really, but it's hard to get me to change. It has no view at all. It's on the street, there's a fire station, and a big building across from it. It's a thin room, cluttered, with nothing on the walls. I have a candle. No, I'm kidding about the candle. It's all very simple; I don't have any rituals.

I tend to write in the morning. Sometimes at night. Whenever my head calms down. If I'm working, I work every day, for five minutes or five hours, it depends where I'm at. If I'm stuck I tend to stop, take a walk, maybe go shopping. I might have half a thought that leads to a thought that I need to have, but it doesn't happen all the time. Sometimes if I'm stuck I'll put on some music, but not very often. I have some music that I've been listening to for a long time, but it's private, sorry. I don't want anyone laughing at my music tastes. Some of it is in *The Sellout*.

I go back and edit bit by bit, by taking a chunk and going through it. I can't go forward unless that chunk is pretty close to where I want it to be. It could be five pages, 10 pages – wherever I get to before I exhale. There's nothing in particular that makes me get on a roll. Sometimes you surprise yourself. It's like rolling dice: you just keep going and keep going and then one of those times it will just come.

Paul Beatty

Haruki Murakami

I got up before five A.M. and went to bed before ten P.M. People are at their best at different times of day, but I'm definitely a morning person. That's when I can focus and finish up important work I have to do.

Afterward I work out or do other errands that don't take much concentration. At the end of the day I relax and don't do any more work. I read, listen to music, take it easy, and try to go to bed early. This is the pattern I've mostly followed up till today. Thanks to this, I've been able to work efficiently these past twenty-four years. It's a lifestyle, though, that doesn't allow for much nightlife, and sometimes your relationships with other people become problematic. Some people even get mad at you, because they invite you to go somewhere or do something with them and you keep turning them down.

I'm struck by how, except when you're young, you really need to prioritize in life, figuring out in what order you should divide up your time and energy. If you don't get that sort of system set by a certain age, you'll lack focus and your life will be out of balance. I placed the highest priority on the sort of life that lets me focus on writing, not associating with all the people around me. I felt that the indispensable relationship I should build in my life was not with a specific person, but with an unspecified number of readers. As long as I got my day-to-day life set so that each work was an improvement over the last, then many of my readers would welcome whatever life I chose for myself. Shouldn't this be my duty as a novelist, and my top priority? My opinion hasn't changed over the years. I can't see my readers' faces, so in a sense it's a conceptual type of human relationship, but I've consistently considered this invisible, conceptual relationship to be the most important thing in my life.

In other words, you can't please everybody.

Beginning a book is unpleasant. I'm entirely uncertain about the character and the predicament, and a character and his predicament is what I have to begin with. Worse than not knowing your subject is not knowing how to treat it, because that's finally everything. I type out beginnings and they're awful, more of an unconscious parody of my previous book than the breakaway from it that I want. I need something driving down the centre of a book, a magnet to draw everything to it – that's what I look for during the first month of writing something new.

Philip Roth

1 .... Abandon the idea that you are ever going to finish. Lose track of the 400 pages and write just one page for each day, it helps. Then when it gets finished, you are always surprised.

2 .... Write freely and as rapidly as possible and throw the whole thing on paper. Never correct or rewrite until the whole thing is down. Rewrite in process is usually found to be an excuse for not going on. It also interferes with flow and rhythm which can only come from a kind of unconscious association with the material.

3 .... Forget your generalized audience. In the first place, the nameless, faceless audience will scare you to death and in the second place, unlike the theater, it doesn't exist. In writing, your audience is one single reader. I have found that sometimes it helps to pick out one person – a real person you know, or an imagined person and write to that one.

4 .... If a scene or a section gets the better of you and you still think you want it – bypass it and go on. When you have finished the whole you can come back to it and then you may find that the reason it gave trouble is because it didn't belong there.

5 .... Beware of a scene that becomes too dear to you, dearer than the rest. It will usually be found that it is out of drawing.

6 .... If you are using dialogue – say it aloud as you write it. Only then will it have the sound of speech.

John Steinbeck

It has become increasingly plain to me that the very excellent organisation of a long book or the finest perceptions and judgement in time of revision do not go well with liquor. A short story can be written on a bottle, but for a novel you need the mental speed that enables you to keep the whole pattern in your head and ruthlessly sacrifice the sideshows as Ernest [Hemingway] did in *A Farewell to Arms*. If a mind is slowed up ever so little it lives in the individual part of a book rather than in a book as a whole; memory is dulled. I would give anything if I hadn't written Part iii of *Tender is the Night* entirely on stimulant. If I had one more crack at it cold sober I believe it might have made a great difference. Even Ernest commented on sections that were needlessly included and as an artist he is as near as I know for a final reference.

F. Scott Fitzgerald

I used to say no [I don't outline] and I think that's a lie. I outlined in certain ways – not the outline that your third-grade teacher taught you to do. Sometimes I write down in a flash form what I think is the overall story structure. They're cryptic notes to myself. Or I'll sit down and write a summary – three to ten pages of what I think it's about. Or I'll write down the movement of a particular chapter. It's good to have that because I can then move to the next part and say, Oh, I needed to include this or that.
Amy Tan

I sometimes wonder whether the act of surrender is not one of the greatest of all – the highest. . . . It 'needs' real humility and at the same time an absolute belief in ones own essential freedom. It is an act of faith. At the last moments like all great acts it is pure risk. This is true for me as a human being and as a writer. Dear Heaven how hard it is to let go – to step into the blue. And yet ones creative life depends on it and one *desires* to do nothing else.
Katherine Mansfield

Geoff Dyer

Over the years I had come across several places that offered the ideal conditions to work. The room in Montepulciano, for example, with the lovely wooden bed and white sheets, the window gazing out over the Tuscan countryside, the terrace formed by what had once been a little bridge connecting our building to the one next door. Or the house in Lauzun with the room overlooking a field of wheat, facing west so that in the evenings the paper on the desk was bathed in red. Or my apartment on Rue Popincourt with the floor-to-ceiling window from which you could see right down Rue de la Roquette, as far as the Bastille almost.

What they all had in common, these ideal places for working, was that I never got any work done in them. I would sit down at my desk and think to myself *What perfect conditions for working*, then I would look out at the sun smouldering over the wheat, or at the trees gathering the Tuscan light around themselves, or at the Parisians walking through the twilight and traffic of Rue de la Roquette, and I would write a few lines like 'If I look up from my desk I can see the sun smouldering over the wheat'; or 'Through my window: crowded twilight on the Rue de la Roquette'; and then, in order to make sure what I was writing was capturing exactly the moment and the mood, I would look up again at the sun smouldering over the flame-red wheat or the crowds moving through the neon twilight of Rue de la Roquette and add a few more words like 'flame-red' or 'neon', and then, in order to give myself totally to the scene, would lay down my pen and simply gaze out at the scene, thinking that it was actually a waste to sit here writing when I could be looking and by looking – especially on Rue de la Roquette where the pedestrians hurrying home in the neon twilight would look up and see a figure at desk, bathed in the yellow light of the anglepoise – actually become part of the scene, whereas writing involved not an immersion in the actual scene but its opposite, a detachment from it. After a very short time I would grow bored by contemplating the scene,

would leave my desk and go for a walk in the wheatfield sunset
or leave my apartment and walk down to the Bastille
so that I could become one of the people walking back
through the neon twilight of the Rue de la Roquette, looking
up at the empty desk, bathed in the light of the anglepoise . . .

When I thought of the ideal conditions for working,
in other words, I looked at things form the perspective of
someone not working, of someone on holiday, of a tourist in
Taormina. I always had in mind the view that my desk would
overlook, thereby overlooking the fact that the view from the
desk is invisible when you are actually working, and forgetting
that of the many genres of sentence I dislike there is none that
I despise more than ones which proceed along the lines of 'If
I look up from desk . . .'. The ideal conditions for working were
actually the worst possible conditions for working.

I just sit down, I put down notes after notes, about 400 pages of
them, practically all of them utterly valueless, and then eventually
one scene would clip onto another scene. It's a bit like doing a
crossword puzzle, you get the clue down and then you have to get
the one across and unless the two fit you can't get any further . . .
I have to know exactly where I'm going before I start a novel,
I have the complete scenario.
P.G. Wodehouse

FAILING

Writer's block and other troubles

I am quite sure that I am not a great novelist because I've only got down onto paper really three types of people. The person who I think I am, the people who irritate me, and the people I'd like to be. When you get to the really great people, like Tolstoy, you find that they can get hold of all types.
E.M. Forster

Ever tried. Ever failed. No matter. Try again. Fail again. Fail better.
Samuel Beckett

Anthony Trollope

But how is a man to know whether or not he has within him the qualities necessary for such a career? He makes an attempt, and fails; repeats his attempt, and fails again! So many have succeeded at last who have failed more than once or twice! Who will tell him the truth as to himself? Who has power to find out that truth? The hard man sends him off without a scruple to that office-stool; the soft man assures him that there is much merit in his manuscript.

I never really understood people who say they have writer's block. It seems to me that the natural remedy to that would be to keep reading. There just isn't an idea there, but no need to be stressed about that. There's this seasonal nature to inspiration that we have to harvest. There's the winter and then the spring, and then wait for the summer for it all to ripen. I'm quite happy in my creative winter.

Eleanor Catton

Although it's terrible to go through, I have great respect for blockage, and I've learned to listen carefully to what it's saying. In my experience, it happens when I'm trying to write something that I'm not ready to write, or that I don't really want to write. And there's no way to discover my unreadiness or unwillingness except to try and fail.

At a certain point, often after months of failure and frustration, I'm forced to stop and undertake a self-analysis through note-taking and conversation with trusted friends. I might then discover that I'm trying to write about a character I don't actually like, or that I'm trying to live up to someone else's expectation of my writing, or that I'm not yet pyschologically prepared to enter the emotional territory I've staked out for myself. Whatever the problem is, the solution is always to find my way back to love, to desire, to pleasure.

Jonathan Franzen

Martin Amis

What sometimes happens is that you get stuck, and it's really not what you're about to do that's stumping you, it's something you've already done that isn't right. You have to go back and fix that. My father described a process in which, as it were, he had to take himself gently but firmly by the hand and say, 'Now all right, calm down. What is it that's worrying you?' The dialogue will go: 'Well, it's the first page, actually. What is it about the first page?' He might say, 'The first sentence.' And he realised that it was only a little thing that was holding him up.

You are better off doing nothing than doing something badly. But the problem is that bad writers tend to have the self-confidence, while the good ones tend to have self-doubt.

Charles Bukowski

It is the nature of the artist to mind excessively what is said about him. Literature is strewn with the wreckage of men who have minded beyond reason the opinions of others.
Virginia Woolf

Gore Vidal

That famous writer's block is a myth as far as I'm concerned. I think bad writers must have a great difficulty writing. They don't want to do it. They have become writers out of reasons of ambition. It must be a great strain to them to make marks on a page when they really have nothing much to say, and don't enjoy doing it. I'm not so sure what I have to say but I certainly enjoy making sentences.

One can think of a life in art . . . in two or perhaps three stages. In the first you find, or pose for yourself, a great question. In the second you labor away at answering it. And then, if you live long enough, you come to the third stage, when the aforesaid great question begins to bore you, and you need to look elsewhere.

J.M. Coetzee

Anne Enright

I have no problem with failure – it is
success that makes me sad. Failure
is easy. I do it every day, I have been
doing it for years. I have thrown out
more sentences than I ever kept, I
have dumped months of work, I have
wasted whole years writing the wrong things for the wrong
people. Even when I am pointed the right way and productive
and finally published, I am not satisfied by the results. This
is not an affectation, failure is what writers do. It is built in.
Your immeasurable ambition is eked out through the many
thousand individual words of your novel, each one of them
written and rewritten several times, and this requires you
to hold your nerve for a very long period of time – or forget
about holding your nerve, forget about the wide world and all
that anxiety and just do it, one word after the other. And then
redo it, so it reads better. The writer's great and sustaining
love is for the language they work with every day. It may not
be what gets us to the desk but it is what keeps us there and,
after 20 or 30 years, this love yields habit and pleasure and
necessity.

So. All this is known. In the long run we are all dead, and
none of us is Proust. You must recognise that failure is 90%
emotion, 10% self-fulfilling reality, and the fact that we are
haunted by it is neither here nor there. The zen of it is that
success and failure are both an illusion, that these illusions
will keep you from the desk, they will spoil your talent; they
will eat away at your life and your sleep and the way you speak
to the people you love.

The problem with this spiritual argument is that success
and failure are also real. You can finish a real book and it can
be published or not, sell or not, be reviewed or not. Each one
of these real events makes it easier or harder to write, publish,
sell the next book. And the next. And the one after that. If
you keep going and stay on the right side of all this, you can
be offered honours and awards, you can be recognised in
the street, you can be recognised in the streets of several

countries, some of which do not have English as a native language. You can get some grumpy fucker to say that your work is not just successful but important, or several grumpy fuckers, and they can say this before you are quite dead. And all this can happen, by the way, whether or not your work is actually good, or still good. Success may be material but is also an emotion – one that is felt, not by you, but by the crowd. This is why we yearn for it, and can not have it, quite. It is not ours to hold.

It took me three years to write three stories for *The Joy Luck Club* and then four months to finish the rest of them. It took me a year and a half to write a draft for the next book. It takes me longer and longer. It took me very long to write *Saving Fish from Drowning* because I got ill and couldn't even write a sentence for a while. For different reasons I get delayed or paralyzed at some point because of the idea that someone's going to read this and it's going to get published and I wonder. Is this truly the book I want to write? Is this truly a book I want to get published and let go out into the world?

Amy Tan

I think of language as an extremely difficult tool to handle. Sometimes it seems impossible. Other times it succeeds in conveying what I'm trying to say, but to call it successful isn't accurate; moreover, it's as if I keep writing even though I know it's going to fail, but it's the only tool I have. It's a relentless dilemma, and I think it's something that a lot of poets experience. Especially in *Greek Lessons*, the protagonist cannot speak and writes poems instead. Each sentence in a language has beauty and baseness, purity and filth, truth and lies, and my novel explores that even more directly. When the weight of words takes over, it is challenging to even speak sometimes. Despite this, we have to continue to speak and write and read. When I lose to my writing, I take a break. I said that I've written for twenty years, but I've sometimes taken a hiatus for a year or two.

Han Kang

In the middle of writing something you go blank and your mind says: 'No, that's it.' You're being warned. Your subconscious is saying 'I don't like you anymore. You're writing about things I don't give a damn for.' You're being political, or you're being socially aware. You're writing things that will benefit the world. To hell with that! I don't write things to benefit the world. If it happens that they do, swell. I didn't set out to do that. I set out to have a hell of a lot of fun.

Ray Bradbury

Writing a book is a bit like surfing . . .
Most of the time you're waiting. And it's
quite pleasant, sitting in the water waiting.
But you are expecting that the result of a
storm over the horizon, in another time zone,
usually, days old, will radiate out in the form
of waves. And eventually, when they show
up, you turn around and ride that energy
to the shore. It's a lovely thing, feeling that
momentum. If you're lucky, it's also about
grace. As a writer, you roll up to the desk
every day, and then you sit there, waiting, in
the hope that something will come over the
horizon. And then you turn around and ride
it, in the form of a story.
Tim Winton

When I'm blocked, which is not a grave thing for me, I continue
with whatever takes my fancy. I may write from the first to the
fifth chapter, then if I'm not enjoying it I skip to number fifteen
and continue from there.

Orhan Pamuk

Philip Pullman

Writer's block . . . a lot of howling nonsense would be avoided if, in every sentence containing the word WRITER, that word was taken out and the word PLUMBER substituted; and the result examined for the sense it makes. Do plumbers get plumber's block? What would you think of a plumber who used that as an excuse not to do any work that day?

The fact is that writing is hard work, and sometimes you don't want to do it, and you can't think of what to write next, and you're fed up with the whole damn business. Do you think plumbers don't feel like that about their work from time to time? Of course there will be days when the stuff is not flowing freely. What you do then is MAKE IT UP. I like the reply of the composer Shostakovich to a student who complained that he couldn't find a theme for his second movement. 'Never mind the theme! Just write the movement!' he said.

Writer's block is a condition that affects amateurs and people who aren't serious about writing. So is the opposite, namely inspiration, which amateurs are also very fond of. Putting it another way: a professional writer is someone who writes just as well when they're not inspired as when they are.

My greatest anxiety at present is that this 4ᵗʰ work shᵈ not disgrace what was good in the others. But on this point I will do myself the justice to declare that whatever may be my wishes for its' success, I am very strongly haunted by the idea that to those Readers who have preferred P&P. it will appear inferior in Wit, & to those who have preferred MP. very inferior in good Sense.

Jane Austen

Alice Munro

I could be writing away one day and think I've done very well; I've done more pages than I usually do. Then I get up the next morning and realize I don't want to work on it anymore. When I have a terrible reluctance to go near it, when I would have to push myself to continue, I generally know that something is badly wrong. Often, in about three quarters of what I do, I reach a point somewhere, fairly early on, when I think I'm going to abandon this story. I get myself through a day or two of bad depression, grouching around. And I think of something else I can write. It's sort of like a love affair: you're getting out of all the disappointment and misery by going out with some new man you don't really like at all, but you haven't noticed that yet. Then, I will suddenly come up with something about the story that I abandoned; I will see how to do it. But that only seems to happen after I've said, No, this isn't going to work, forget it . . .

Sometimes I can't, and I spend the whole day in a very bad mood. That's the only time I'm really irritable. If Gerry talks to me or keeps going in and out of the room or bangs around a lot, I am on edge and enraged. And if he sings or something like that, it's terrible. I'm trying to think something through, and I'm just running into brick walls; I'm not getting through it. Generally I'll do that for a while before I'll give it up. This whole process might take up to a week, the time of trying to think it through, trying to retrieve it, then giving it up and thinking about something else, and then getting it back, usually quite unexpectedly, when I'm in the grocery store or out for a drive. I'll think, Oh well, I have to do it from the point of view of so-and-so, and I have to cut this character out, and of course these people are not married, or whatever. The big change, which is usually the radical change . . .

I don't even know if it makes the story better. What it does is make it possible for me to continue to write. That's what I mean by saying I don't think I have this overwhelming thing that comes in and dictates to me. I only seem to get a grasp on what I want to write about with the greatest difficulty. And barely.

127

There's enormous pleasure in working out plots.
But writing can be as painful as childbirth. I threw
away not just my first, but my second novel.
Angela Carter

Ring Lardner

A good many young writers make the
mistake of enclosing a stamped, self-
addressed envelope, big enough for the
manuscript to come back in. That is too
much of a temptation to the editor.

Dear Sir,

I have looked at the larger half of the first volume of your novel, and have pursued the more difficult points of the story through the other two volumes.

You will, of course, receive my opinion as that of an individual writer and student of art, who by no means claims to be infallible.

I think you are too ambitious, and that you have not sufficient knowledge of life or character to venture on so comprehensive an attempt. Evidences of inexperience in every way, and of your power being far below the situations that you imagine, present themselves to me in almost every page I have read. It would greatly surprise me if you found a publisher for this story, on trying your fortune in that line, or derived anything from it but weariness and bitterness of spirit.

On the evidence thus put before me, I cannot even entirely satisfy myself that you have the faculty of authorship latent within you. If you have not, and yet pursue a vocation towards which you have no call, you cannot choose but be a wretched man. Let me counsel you to have the patience to form yourself carefully, and the courage to renounce the endeavour if you cannot establish your case on a very much smaller scale. You see around you every day, how many outlets there are for short pieces of fiction in all kinds. Try if you can achieve any success within these modest limits (I have practised in my time what I preach to you), and in the meantime put your three volumes away.

Faithfully yours.
Charles Dickens

Junot Díaz

It wasn't that I couldn't write. I wrote every day. I actually worked really hard at writing. At my desk by 7 A.M., would work a full eight and more. Scribbled at the dinner table, in bed, on the toilet, on the No. 6 train, at Shea Stadium. I did everything I could. But none of it worked. My novel, which I had started with such hope shortly after publishing my first book of stories, wouldn't budge past the 75-page mark. Nothing I wrote past page 75 made any kind of sense. Nothing. Which would have been fine if the first 75 pages hadn't been pretty damn cool. But they were cool, showed a lot of promise. Would also have been fine if I could have just jumped to something else. But I couldn't. All the other novels I tried sucked worse than the stalled one, and even more disturbing, I seemed to have lost the ability to write short stories. It was like I had somehow slipped into a No-Writing Twilight Zone and I couldn't find an exit. Like I'd been chained to the sinking ship of those 75 pages and there was no key and no patching the hole in the hull. I wrote and I wrote and I wrote, but nothing I produced was worth a damn.

Want to talk about stubborn? I kept at it for five straight years. Five damn years. Every day failing for five years? I'm a pretty stubborn, pretty hard-hearted character, but those five years of fail did a number on my psyche. On me. Five years, 60 months? It just about wiped me out. By the end of that fifth year, perhaps in an attempt to save myself, to escape my despair, I started becoming convinced that I had written all I had to write, that I was a minor league Ralph Ellison, a Pop Warner Edward Rivera, that maybe it was time, for the sake of my mental health, for me to move on to another profession, and if the inspiration struck again some time in the future . . . well, great. But I knew I couldn't go on much more the way I was going. I just couldn't. I was living with my fiancée at the time (over now, another terrible story) and was so depressed and self-loathing I could barely function. . . . I put the manuscript away. All the hundreds of failed pages boxed, and hidden in the closet. I think I cried as I did it. . . .

One night in August, unable to sleep, sickened that I was giving up, but even more frightened by the thought of having to return to the writing, I dug out the manuscript. I figured if I could find one good thing in the pages I would go back to it. Just one good thing. Like flipping a coin, I'd let the pages decide. Spent the whole night reading everything I had written, and guess what? It was still terrible. In fact with the new distance the lameness was even worse than I'd thought. That's when I should have put everything in the box. When I should have turned my back and trudged into my new life. I didn't have the heart to go on. But I guess I did. While my fiancée slept, I separated the 75 pages that were worthy from the mountain of loss, sat at my desk, and despite every part of me shrieking no no no no, I jumped back down the rabbit hole again. There were no sudden miracles. It took two more years of heartbreak, of being utterly, dismayingly lost before the novel I had dreamed about for all those years finally started revealing itself. And another three years after that before I could look up from my desk and say the word I'd wanted to say for more than a decade: done.

That's my tale in a nutshell. Not the tale of how I came to write my novel but rather of how I became a writer. Because, in truth, I didn't become a writer the first time I put pen to paper or when I finished my first book (easy) or my second one (hard). You see, in my view a writer is a writer not because she writes well and easily, because she has amazing talent, because everything she does is golden. In my view a writer is a writer because even when there is no hope, even when nothing you do shows any sign of promise, you keep writing anyway. Wasn't until that night when I was faced with all those lousy pages that I realized, really realized, what it was exactly that I am.

The scariest moment is always just before you start.
After that, things can only get better.
Stephen King

If writing were not difficult it wouldn't be enjoyable. If it were too easy you can feel you haven't quite grasped the story, that you have omitted something essential. But the difficulty is more likely to be internal to the work itself – where it should be – rather than in some personal crisis. I'm not sure you become more fluent as you get older, but you become less fearful of imagined consequences. There has to be a lot to clear away, then the work starts.

Hanif Kureishi

Failure is just another name for much of real life: much of what we set out to accomplish ends in failure, at least in our own eyes. Who set the bar so high that most of our attempts to sail gracefully over it on the viewless wings of Poesy end in an undignified scramble or a nasty fall into the mud? Who told us we had to succeed at any cost?

But my own personal failure list? It's a long one. Sewing failures, to begin with. The yellow shortie coat with the lopsided hem I crafted when I was 12? It made me look like a street waif, and caused my mother to hide her eyes every time I ventured out the door in it. Or maybe you'd prefer a few academic failures? My bad Latin mark in Grade 12, my 51 in Algebra? Or my failure to learn touch-typing: now that had consequences.

But such adolescent slippages come within the normal range. Something more epic, perhaps? A failed novel? Much time expended, many floor-pacings and scribblings, nothing achieved; or, as they say in Newfoundland, a wet arse and no fish caught…

Get back on the horse that threw you, as they used to say. They also used to say: you learn as much from failure as you learn from success.
Margaret Atwood

Ursula K. Le Guin

Beginners' failures are often the result of trying to work with strong feelings and ideas without having found the images to embody them, or without even knowing how to find the words and string them together. Ignorance of English vocabulary and grammar is a considerable liability to a writer of English. The best cure for it is, I believe, reading. People who learned to talk at two or so and have been practicing talking ever since feel with some justification that they know their language; but what they know is their spoken language, and if they read little, or read schlock, and haven't written much, their writing is going to be pretty much what their talking was when they were two.

Edith Wharton

I was much helped by Walter Berry. No critic was ever severer, but none had more respect for the artist's liberty. He taught me never to be satisfied with my own work, but never to let my inward conviction as to the rightness of anything I had done be affected by outside opinion. I remember, after writing the first chapters of 'The Valley of Decision', which I had begun in a burst of lyric rapture and didn't know how to go on with, confessing to him my difficulty and my discouragement. He looked through what I had written, handed it back, and said simply: 'Don't worry about how you're to go on. Just write down everything you feel like telling.' The advice freed me once for all from the incubus of an artificially pre-designed plan, and sent me rushing ahead with my tale, letting each incident create the next, and keeping in sight only the novelist's essential sign-post; the inner significance of the 'case' selected. Yet when the novel was done, I remember how meticulously he studied it from the point of view of language, marking down faulty syntax and false metaphors, smiling away over-emphasis and unnecessary repetitions, helping me patiently through the beginner's verbal perplexities, yet never laying hands on what he considered sacred: the SOUL of the novel, which is (or should be) the writer's own soul.

Someone asked me the other day about writer's block. Writer's block basically doesn't exist. It's a way of saying the writing you are trying to do came out so badly you're not willing to go through with it. So it's not about being blocked, it's about being unwilling to persevere with really bad-quality writing. My feeling is you should always go through that, because it's part and parcel of writing. If you're digging for gold, you sift a lot of crap.

Joe Dunthorne

Lionel Shriver

As if the story of the book itself were fated to duplicate the story inside the book, my sixth novel, *Double Fault*, was purchased by Doubleday in 1997 with great fanfare, yet in hardback sold so poorly that no house bid for the paperback until many years later. At core, that book is about failure – a subject about which, as a struggling writer, I'd grown depressingly expert. Hungry for both fantasy and inspiration, readers crave protagonists who, after overcoming seemingly insurmountable obstacles, triumph at the end of the day. No one wanted to buy a book about disappointment.

Yet most people fail. In the big picture, few of our careers live up to the dreams we nursed when we were young. In fact, one underside of success is that it's nearly always penultimate, and so every accomplishment merely raises the bar. Each new success conjures new standards we can't meet, thereby inventing ingenious new ways to fail. I've not been awarded the Nobel Prize for Literature, and may never be. My latest novel missed the Times top 10 bestseller list by 46 copies. Most of the reviews were good, but they weren't all good. It's a doddle to locate a perspective from which I am still failing.

Even in the little picture, failure is commonplace. Our team loses the pub quiz, or we're slaughtered in a game of squash. A job interview goes badly, or we burn the lasagne. A joke falls flat. Letting ourselves down in some fashion is such an integral part of daily life that the paucity of literature on the subject is baffling. There are scads of self-help books on how to succeed, but I've never come across a single one on how to contend with not succeeding – which is more the form for practically everybody, right?

I'm fascinated by failure, a far more difficult experience to ride out with grace than victory, which tends to bring out the best in all but gloating arseholes: magnanimity, generosity, ease, confidence, joy, relaxation, energy, festivity, and a positive outlook. In contrast, failure naturally elicits bitterness, resentment, dolour, enervation, listlessness, pessimism and low self-esteem – a pretty ugly package.

Yet, against the odds, it's possible to fail well – to rise above the unpleasant basket of emotions that come with the territory

and to not allow disappointment to sour one's very soul. I am bowled over by the massive number of remarkable people who face down the fact that no, they are not going to be film directors, famous artists or billionaire entrepreneurs and still come out the other side as cheerful, decent, gracious human beings. As emotional achievements go, that is much more impressive than making a go of something and avoiding becoming a complete jerk.

The trajectory of my own career as a novelist is sometimes held up as an example of perseverance, since six commercial duds were finally followed by a proper bestseller. Looking back, I'm torn on whether for a dozen years I 'failed well'. I was often glum, and I nursed my share of resentments. But I guess I still made my partner a decent dinner every night, and I wasn't relentlessly crap company. I kept writing books, even if no one bought them. Because my black years were artistically productive, it's tempting to romanticise them. That would be a mistake.

I do think that very early success is more bane than boon, and not having had my career handed to me on a plate must have been good for me, not only as a writer but as a person. Nevertheless, those were dark times – getting my hopes up for one manuscript after another and having them dashed. It wasn't ennobling. True, after having carved out a little place for myself in the world, I am probably a warmer woman with a lighter spirit, but that may not be to my credit. We celebrate success, hope for the best, and admire determination. So we shy from acknowledging that there's a point at which it's pretty clear that whatever it is we're so determined to achieve is not going to happen. In which case, why keep beating our heads against the wall? There's something to be said for giving up. Hell, maybe there's such a thing as 'giving up well', too.

If you get stuck, get away from your desk. Take a walk, take a bath, go to sleep, make a pie, draw, listen to music, meditate, exercise; whatever you do, don't just stick there scowling at the problem. But don't make telephone calls or go to a party; if you do, other people's words will pour in where your lost words should be. Open a gap for them, create a space. Be patient.

Hilary Mantel

Perhaps it would be better not to be a writer, but if you must, then write. If all feels hopeless, if that famous 'inspiration' will not come, write. If you are a genius, you'll make your own rules, but if not – and the odds are against it – go to your desk no matter what your mood, face the icy challenge of the paper – write.
J.B. Priestley

[It's so important to be] willing to write really badly. It won't hurt you to do that. I think there is this fear of writing badly, something primal about it, like: 'This bad stuff is coming out of me . . .' Forget it! Let it float away and the good stuff follows. For me, the bad beginning is just something to build on. It's no big deal. You have to give yourself permission to do that because you can't expect to write regularly and always write well. That's when people get into the habit of waiting for the good moments, and that is where I think writer's block comes from. Like: It's not happening. Well, maybe good writing isn't happening, but let some bad writing happen. Let it happen! I mean, when I was writing *The Keep*, my writing was so terrible. It was God-awful. My working title for that first draft was, *A Short Bad Novel*. I thought: 'How can I disappoint?'

So, just write and be happy that you did it. You stuck to the routine. You're kind of holding the place so that you're present for when something good is ready to come.

And then it's all about rewriting. Re-visiting, re-visiting and re-writing. I think it's a mistake to be too precious about one's words. I feel the same way about the criticism. You're not going to break! It's pretty tough to stick it out, to do this. So, get used to it! People are going to not like it. Okay! You'll live. So, it's bad. Okay. You'll live! They said 'no.' You know what? Everyone gets said 'no' to a thousand times. If that is really something that you can't tolerate, this may not work.

Jennifer Egan

H.G. Wells

If you are experiencing difficulties with a book, try the element of surprise: attack it at an hour when it isn't expecting it.

Read over your composition and, when you meet a passage which you think is particularly fine, strike it out.
Samuel Johnson

One of the most difficult things is the first paragraph. I have spent many months on a first paragraph, and once I get it, the rest just comes out very easily.
Gabriel García Márquez

Writer's block is my unconscious mind telling me that something I've just written is either unbelievable or unimportant to me, and I solve it by going back and reinventing some part of what I've already written so that when I write it again, it is believable and interesting to me. Then I can go on. Writer's block is never solved by forcing oneself to 'write through it', because you haven't solved the problem that caused your unconscious mind to rebel against the story, so it still won't work – for you or for the reader.

Orson Scott Card

Writing about a writer's block is better than not writing at all.
Charles Bukowski

Maya Angelou

What I try to do is write. I may write for two weeks 'the cat sat on the mat, that is that, not a rat'. And it might be just the most boring and awful stuff. But I try. When I'm writing, I write. And then it's as if the muse is convinced that I'm serious and says, 'Okay. Okay. I'll come.'

You wanted an update. Here's the update. You won't like it.
THE WINDS OF WINTER is not finished.

Believe me, it gave me no pleasure to type those words.

You're disappointed, and you're not alone. My editors and publishers are disappointed, HBO is disappointed, my agents and foreign publishers and translators are disappointed . . . but no one could possibly be more disappointed than me. For months now I have wanted nothing so much as to be able to say, 'I have completed and delivered THE WINDS OF WINTER' on or before the last day of 2015.

But the book's not done.

Nor is it likely to be finished tomorrow, or next week. Yes, there's a lot written. Hundreds of pages. Dozens of chapters. (Those 'no pages done' reports were insane, the usual garbage internet journalism that I have learned to despise). But there's also a lot still left to write. I am months away still . . . and that's if the writing goes well. (Sometimes it does. Sometimes it doesn't.) Chapters still to write, of course . . . but also rewriting. I always do a lot of rewriting, sometimes just polishing, sometimes pretty major restructures . . .

Look, I have always had problems with deadlines. For whatever reason, I don't respond well to them. Back in November, when I returned to Northwestern to accept my Alumni Award, I told the Medill students that was why I started writing fiction instead of getting a job on a newspaper. I knew even then that daily deadlines would kill me. That was a joke, of course . . . but there was truth in it too. I wrote my first novel, DYING OF THE LIGHT, without a contract and without a deadline. No one even knew I was writing a novel until I sent the completed book to Kirby to sell. I wrote FEVRE DREAM the same way. I wrote THE ARMAGEDDON RAG the same way. No contracts, no deadlines, no one waiting. Write at my own pace and deliver when I'm done. That's really how I am most comfortable, even now.

But I won't make excuses. . . .

It will be done when it's done. And it will be as good as I can possibly make it. . . .

Current Location: Santa Fe

Current Mood: Depressed

Tags: a song of ice and fire, game of thrones, publishing, writing

Neil Gaiman

In my experience, writer's block is very real. You'll be writing
something and suddenly it stops. The characters stop talking.
You've been happily just transcribing everything they've been
saying, and suddenly they sit down and shut up. Suddenly, you
are in deep trouble. It does happen. It's very real.

It's not something (in my experience anyway) that happens
on everything at the same time. It's just that sometimes a project
needs a little time to think, a little time to breathe. So what I tend
to do when that happens is I always have two or three other things
that I'm doing at the same time. I can just go to one of the ones
that's working . . .

The other thing that I would say about writer's block is that it
can be very, very subjective. By which I mean, you can have one of
those days when you sit down and every word is crap. It is awful.
You cannot understand how or why you are writing, what gave you
the illusion or delusion that you would every have anything to say
that anybody would ever want to listen to. You're not quite sure
why you're wasting your time. And if there is one thing you're sure
of, it's that everything that is being written that day is rubbish.
I would also note that on those days (especially if deadlines and
things are involved) is that I keep writing. The following day,
when I actually come to look at what has been written, I will
usually look at what I did the day before, and think, 'That's not
quite as bad as I remember. All I need to do is delete that line and
move that sentence around and its fairly usable. It's not that bad.'

I have a fantasy, which I've often spoken of, that I am walking past a bookshop and click my fingers and by magic my books on the shelves inside all go blank, so that I might start over and rewrite them. Impossible to go back, of course. One writes what one writes, and is stuck with it.

John Banville

I scarcely look with full satisfaction upon any [of my books]; for they do not seem what they might have been. I often wish that I could have twenty years more to take them down from the shelf one by one, and write them over.

Washington Irving

I am alone in the privacy of my faded blue room with my sick cat, the bare February branches waving at the window, an ironic paper weight that says Business is Good, a New England conscience developed in Minnesota and my greatest problem:

'Shall I run it out? Or shall I turn back?'

Shall I say:

'I know I had something to prove, and it may develop farther along in the story?'

Or else:

'This is just bullheadedness – better throw it away and start over.'

The latter is one of the most difficult decisions that an author must make – to make it philosophically, before he has exhausted himself in a hundred-hour effort to resuscitate a corpse or disentangle innumerable wet snarls, is a test of whether or not he is really a professional. There are often occasions when such a decision is doubly difficult. In the last stages of a novel, for instance, where there is no question of junking the whole, but when an entire favorite character has to be hauled out by the heels, screeching, and dragging half a dozen good scenes with him.

F. Scott Fitzgerald

All the books I have ever written fill me
only with a complex feeling of repentance.
Jorge Luis Borges

THE ART OF WRITING

Searching for words

Walter Scott

Every successful novelist must be more or less
a poet, even though he may never have written
a line of verse. The quality of imagination is
absolutely indispensable to him; his accurate
power of examining and embodying human
character and human passion, as well as the
external face of nature, is not less essential;
and the talent of describing well what he feels
with acuteness, added to the above requisites,
goes far to complete the poetic character.

The task of an author is, either to teach what is not known, or to recommend known truths by his manner of adorning them; either to let new light in upon the mind, and open new scenes to the prospect, or to vary the dress and situation of common objects, so as to give them fresh grace and more powerful attractions, to spread such flowers over the regions through which the intellect has already made its progress, as may tempt it to return, and take a second view of things hastily passed over, or negligently regarded.

Samuel Johnson

To produce a mighty book,
you must choose a mighty theme.
No great and enduring volume
can ever be written on the flea,
though many there be who
have tried it.
Herman Melville

Writers take words seriously – perhaps the last professional class that does – and they struggle to steer their own through the crosswinds of meddling editors and careless typesetters and obtuse and malevolent reviewers into the lap of the ideal reader.
John Updike

A writer – and, I believe, generally all persons – must think that whatever happens to him or her is a resource. All things have been given to us for a purpose, and an artist must feel this more intensely. All that happens to us, including our humiliations, our misfortunes, our embarrassments, all is given to us as raw material, as clay, so that we may shape our art.

I should say that unhappiness is one of the many tools given to the writer. Or one of the many materials, for another metaphor. Unhappiness, solitude, all those should be used by the writer. Even the nightmare is a tool. Many of my stories have been given to me by nightmares. I have a nightmare every other night.

Jorge Luis Borges

Whether it is right or advisable to create
beings like Heathcliff, I do not know:
I scarcely think it is. But this I know: the
writer who possesses the creative gift owns
something of which he is not always master –
something that, at times, strangely wills and
works for itself. He may lay down rules and
devise principles, and to rules and principles
it will perhaps for years lie in subjection;
and then, haply without any warning of revolt,
there comes a time when it will no longer
consent to 'harrow the valleys, or be bound
with a band in the furrow' – when it 'laughs
at the multitude of the city, and regards not
the crying of the driver' – when, refusing
absolutely to make ropes out of sea-sand
any longer, it sets to work on statue-hewing,
and you have a Pluto or a Jove, a Tisiphone
or a Psyche, a Mermaid or a Madonna, as
Fate or Inspiration direct. Be the work grim
or glorious, dread or divine, you have little
choice left but quiescent adoption. As for you
– the nominal artist – your share in it has been
to work passively under dictates you neither
delivered nor could question – that would
not be uttered at your prayer, nor suppressed
nor changed at your caprice. If the result be
attractive, the World will praise you, who little
deserve praise; if it be repulsive, the same
World will blame you, who almost as little
deserve blame.
Charlotte Brontë

Having gone through your MS. (which I should have done sooner, but that I have not been very well), I write these few following words about it . . .

Of the story itself I honestly say that I think highly. The style is particularly easy and agreeable . . . But it strikes me that you constantly hurry your narrative (and yet without getting on) *by telling it, in a sort of impetuous breathless way, in your own person, when the people should tell it and act it for themselves.* My notion always is, that when I have made the people to play out the play, it is, as it were, their business to do it, and not mine. Then, unless you really have led up to a great situation like Basil's death, you are bound in art to make more of it. Such a scene should form a chapter of itself. Impressed upon the reader's memory, it would go far to make the fortune of the book. Suppose yourself telling that affecting incident in a letter to a friend. Wouldn't you describe how you went through the life and stir of the streets and roads to the sick-room? Wouldn't you say what kind of room it was, what time of day it was, whether it was sunlight, starlight, or moonlight? Wouldn't you have a strong impression on your mind of how you were received, when you first met the look of the dying man, what strange contrasts were about you and struck you? I don't want you, in a novel, to present *yourself* to tell such things, but I want the things to be there. You make no more of the situation than the index might, or a descriptive playbill might in giving a summary of the tragedy under representation.

Charles Dickens

I have always held the old-fashioned opinion that the primary object of a work of fiction should be to tell a story; and I have never believed that the novelist who properly performed this first condition of his art, was in danger, on that account, of neglecting the delineation of character – for this plain reason, that the effect produced by any narrative of events is essentially dependent, not on the events themselves, but on the human interest which is directly connected with them. It may be possible, in novel-writing, to present characters successfully without telling a story; but it is not possible to tell a story successfully without presenting characters: their existence, as recognizable realities, being the sole condition on which the story can be effectively told. The only narrative which can hope to lay a strong hold on the attention of readers, is a narrative which interests them about men and women – for the perfectly obvious reason that they are men and women themselves.

Wilkie Collins

It must always be borne in mind, despite the claims of realism, that the best fiction, like the highest artistic expression in other modes, is more true, so to put it, then [*sic*] history or nature can be.

Thomas Hardy

George Eliot

What is the best way of telling a story? Since the standard must be the interest of the audience, there must be several or many good ways rather than one best. For we get interested in the stories life presents to us through divers orders and modes of presentation. Very commonly our first awakening to a desire of knowing a man's past or future comes from our seeing him as a stranger in some unusual or pathetic or humorous situation, or manifesting some remarkable characteristics. We make inquiries in consequence, or we become observant and attentive whenever opportunities of knowing more may happen to present themselves without our search.

You have seen a refined face among the prisoners picking tow in gaol; you afterwards see the same unforgettable face in a pulpit: he must be of dull fibre who would not care to know more about a life which showed such contrasts, though he might gather his knowledge in a fragmentary and unchronological way.

Again, we have heard much, or at least something not quite common, about a man whom we have never seen, and hence we look round with curiosity when we are told that he is present; whatever he says or does before us is charged with a meaning due to our previous hearsay knowledge about him, gathered either from dialogue of which he was expressly and emphatically the subject, or from incidental remark, or from general report either in or out of print.

These indirect ways of arriving at knowledge are always the most stirring even in relation to impersonal subjects. To see a chemical experiment gives an attractiveness to a definition of chemistry, and fills it with a significance which it would never have had without the pleasant shock of an unusual sequence, such as the transformation of a solid into gas, and vice versa. To see a word for the first time either as substantive or adjective in a connection where we care about knowing its complete meaning, is the way to vivify its meaning in our recollection. Curiosity becomes the more eager from the incompleteness of the first information.

1	....	Never open a book with weather.
2	....	Avoid prologues.
3	....	Never use a verb other than 'said' to carry dialogue.
4	....	Never use an adverb to modify the verb 'said' . . . he admonished gravely.
5	....	Keep your exclamation points under control. You are allowed no more than two or three per 100,000 words of prose.
6	....	Never use the words 'suddenly' or 'all hell broke loose'.
7	....	Use regional dialect, patois, sparingly.
8	....	Avoid detailed descriptions of characters.
9	....	Don't go into great detail describing places and things.
10	....	Try to leave out the part that readers tend to skip.

My most important rule is one that sums up the 10. If it sounds like writing, I rewrite it.
Elmore Leonard

I notice that you use plain, simple language, short words and brief sentences. That is the way to write English – it is the modern way and the best way. Stick to it; don't let fluff and flowers and verbosity creep in. When you catch an adjective, kill it. No, I don't mean utterly, but kill most of them – then the rest will be valuable. They weaken when they are close together. They give strength when they are wide apart. An adjective habit, or a wordy, diffuse, flowery habit, once fastened upon a person, is as hard to get rid of as any other vice.

Mark Twain

There are two very clear indications of real science and real art: the first inner sign is that a scholar or an artist works not for profit, but for sacrifice, for his calling; the second, outer sign is that his works are understandable to all people. Real science studies and makes accessible that knowledge which people at that period of history think important, and real art transfers this truth from the domain of knowledge to the domain of feelings.

Creating art is not as elevated a thing as many people guess, but certainly it is a useful and kind thing to do, especially if it brings people together and arouses kind feelings in them.

Leo Tolstoy

Robert Louis Stevenson

To make a character at all – so to select, so to describe a few acts, a few speeches, perhaps (though this is quite superfluous) a few details of physical appearance, as that these shall all cohere and strike in the reader's mind a common note of personality – there is no more delicate enterprise, success is nowhere less comprehensible than here. We meet a man, we find his talk to have been racy; and yet if every word were taken down by short-hand, we should stand amazed at its essential insignificance. Physical presence, the speaking eye, the inimitable commentary of the voice, it was in these the spell resided; and these are all excluded from the pages of the novel.

There is one writer of fiction whom I have the advantage of knowing; and he confesses to me that his success in this matter (small though it be) is quite surprising to himself. 'In one of my books,' he writes, 'and in one only, the characters took the bit in their mouth; all at once, they became detached from the flat paper, they turned their backs on me and walked off bodily; and from that time, my task was stenographic – it was they who spoke, it was they who wrote the remainder of the story. When this miracle of genesis occurred, I was thrilled with joyous surprise; I felt a certain awe – shall we call it superstitious? And yet how small a miracle it was; with what a partial life were my characters endowed; and when all was said, how little did I know of them! It was a form of words that they supplied me with; it was in a form of words that they consisted; beyond and behind was nothing.' The limitation, which this writer felt and which he seems to have deplored, can be remarked in the work of even literary princes. I think it was Hazlitt who declared that, if the names were dropped at press, he could restore any speech in Shakespeare to the proper speaker; and I dare say we could all pick out the words of Nym or Pistol, Caius or Evans; but not even Hazlitt could do the like for the great leading characters, who yet are cast in a more delicate mould, and appear before us far more subtly and far more fully differentiated, than these easy-going ventriloquial puppets. It is just when the obvious expedients of the barrel organ vocabulary, the droll mispronunciation or the racy dialect, are laid aside, that the true masterpieces are wrought (it would seem) from nothing.

I was working on the proof of one of my poems all the morning, and took out a comma. In the afternoon I put it back again.
Oscar Wilde

Edgar Allen Poe

Nothing is more clear than that every plot, worth the name, must be elaborated to its denouement before anything be attempted with the pen. It is only with the denouement constantly in view that we can give a plot its indispensable air of consequence, or causation, by making the incidents, and especially the tone at all points, tend to the development of the intention.

There is a busybody on your staff who devotes a lot of time to chasing split infinitives. Every good literary craftsman splits his infinitives when the sense demands it. I call for the immediate dismissal of this pedant. It is of no consequence whether he decides to go quickly, or quickly to go, or to quickly go. The important thing is that he should go at once.

George Bernard Shaw

William Makepeace Thackery

Perhaps the lovers of 'excitement' may care to know, that this book began with a very precise plan, which was entirely put aside. Ladies and gentlemen, you were to have been treated, and the writer's and the publisher's pocket benefited, by the recital of the most active horrors. What more exciting than a ruffian (with many admirable virtues) in St Giles's, visited constantly by a young lady from Belgravia? What more stirring than the contrasts of society? the mixture of slang and fashionable language? the escapes, the battles, the murders? Nay, up to nine o'clock this very morning, my poor friend, Colonel Altamont, was doomed to execution, and the author only relented when his victim was actually at the window.

The 'exciting' plan was laid aside (with a very honourable forbearance on the part of the publishers), because, on attempting it, I found that I failed from want of experience of my subject; and never having been intimate with any convict in my life, and the manners of ruffians and gaol-birds being quite unfamiliar to me, the idea of entering into competition with M. Eugene Sue was abandoned. To describe a real rascal, you must make him so horrible that he would be too hideous to show; and unless the painter paints him fairly, I hold he has no right to show him at all.

For your born writer, nothing is so healing as the realization that he has come upon the right word.
Catherine Drinker Bowen

People have often asked me whether I knew the end of a Holmes story before I started it. Of course I do. One could not possibly steer a course if one did not know one's destination. The first thing is to get your idea. Having got that key idea one's next task is to conceal it and lay emphasis upon everything which can make for a different explanation. Holmes, however, can see all the fallacies of the alternatives, and arrives more or less dramatically at the true solution by steps which he can describe and justify. He shows his powers by what the South Americans now call 'Sherlockholmitos', which means clever little deductions, which often have nothing to do with the matter in hand, but impress the reader with a general sense of power. The same effect is gained by his offhand allusion to other cases. Heaven knows how many titles I have thrown about in a casual way, and how many readers have begged me to satisfy their curiosity as to 'Rigoletto and his abominable wife', 'The Adventure of the Tired Captain', or 'The Curious Experience of the Patterson Family in the Island of Uffa'. Once or twice, as in 'The Adventure of the Second Stain', which in my judgment is one of the neatest of the stories, I did actually use the title years before I wrote a story to correspond.
Arthur Conan Doyle

To a chemist, nothing on earth is unclean. A writer must be as objective as a chemist; he must abandon the subjective line; he must know that the dungheap plays a very respectable part in the landscape, and that evil passions are as inherent in life as good ones.
Anton Chekhov

F. Scott Fitzgerald

When a first rate author wants an exquisite heroine or a lovely morning, he finds all the superlatives have been worn shoddy by his inferiors. It should be a rule that bad writers must start with plain heroines and ordinary mornings, and, if they are able, work up to something better.

Art, it seems to me, should simplify. That, indeed, is very nearly the whole of the higher artistic process; finding what conventions of form and what detail one can do without and yet preserve the spirit of the whole – so that all that one has suppressed and cut away is there to the reader's consciousness as much as if it were in type on the page. Millet had done hundreds of sketches of peasants sowing grain, some of them very complicated and interesting, but when he came to paint the spirit of them all into one picture, 'The Sower', the composition is so simple that it seems inevitable. All the discarded sketches that went before made the picture what it finally became, and the process was all the time one of simplifying, of sacrificing many conceptions good in themselves for one that was better and more universal.

Any first rate novel or story must have in it the strength of a dozen fairly good stories that have been sacrificed to it. A good workman can't be a cheap workman; he can't be stingy about wasting material, and he cannot compromise.

Willa Cather

Vladimir Nabokov

There are three points of view from which a writer can be considered: he may be considered as a storyteller, as a teacher, and as an enchanter. A major writer combines these three – storyteller, teacher, enchanter – but it is the enchanter in him that predominates and makes him a major writer.

To the storyteller we turn for entertainment, for mental excitement of the simplest kind, for emotional participation, for the pleasure of traveling in some remote region in space or time. A slightly different though not necessarily higher mind looks for the teacher in the writer. Propagandist, moralist, prophet – this is the rising sequence. We may go to the teacher not only for moral education but also for direct knowledge, for simple facts. . . . Finally, and above all, a great writer is always a great enchanter, and it is here that we come to the really exciting part when we try to grasp the individual magic of his genius and to study the style, the imagery, the pattern of his novels or poems.

The three facets of the great writer – magic, story, lesson – are prone to blend in one impression of unified and unique radiance, since the magic of art may be present in the very bones of the story, in the very marrow of thought. There are masterpieces of dry, limpid, organized thought which provoke in us an artistic quiver quite as strongly as a novel like *Mansfield Park* does or as any rich flow of Dickensian sensual imagery. It seems to me that a good formula to test the quality of a novel is, in the long run, a merging of the precision of poetry and the intuition of science. In order to bask in that magic a wise reader reads the book of genius not with his heart, not so much with his brain, but with his spine. It is there that occurs the telltale tingle even though we must keep a little aloof, a little detached when reading. Then with a pleasure which is both sensual and intellectual we shall watch the artist build his castle of cards and watch the castle of cards become a castle of beautiful steel and glass.

No aspiring author should content himself with a mere acquisition of technical rules. . . . All attempts at gaining literary polish must begin with judicious reading, and the learner must never cease to hold this phase uppermost. In many cases, the usage of good authors will be found a more effective guide than any amount of precept. A page of Addison or of Irving will teach more of style than a whole manual of rules, whilst a story of Poe's will impress upon the mind a more vivid notion of powerful and correct description and narration than will ten dry chapters of a bulky textbook.

In fictional narration, verisimilitude is absolutely essential. A story must be consistent and must contain no event glaringly removed from the usual order of things, unless that event is the main incident, and is approached with the most careful preparation. In real life, odd and erratic things do occasionally happen; but they are out of place in an ordinary story, since fiction is a sort of idealization of the average. Development should be as lifelike as possible, and a weak, trickling conclusion should be assiduously avoided. The end of a story must be stronger rather than weaker than the beginning; since it is the end which contains the denouement or culmination, and which will leave the strongest impression upon the reader. It would not be amiss for the novice to write the last paragraph of his story first, once a synopsis of the plot has been carefully prepared – as it always should be. In this way he will be able to concentrate his freshest mental vigour upon the most important part of his narrative; and if any changes be later found needful, they can easily be made. In no part of a narrative should a grand or emphatic thought or passage be followed by one of tame or prosaic quality. This is anticlimax, and exposes a writer to much ridicule.
H.P. Lovecraft

The important thing is not what we write, but how we write, and in my opinion the modern writer must be an adventurer above all, willing to take every risk, and be prepared to founder in his effort if need be. In other words we must write dangerously. . . . I know when I was writing *Ulysses* I tried to give the colour and tone of Dublin with my words; the drab, yet glistening atmosphere of Dublin, its hallucinatory vapours, its tattered confusion, the atmosphere of its bars, its social immobility – they could only be conveyed by the texture of my words. Thought and plot are not so important as some would make them out to be. The object of any work of art is the transference of emotion; talent is the gift of conveying that emotion. . . . In *Ulysses* I tried to keep close to fact. There is humour of course, for though man's position in this world is fundamentally tragic it can also be seen as humorous. The disparity of what he wants to be and what he is, is no doubt laughable, so much so that a comedian has only to come on to the stage and trip and everyone roars with laughter.

James Joyce

Blot out, correct, insert, refine
Enlarge, diminish, interline
Be mindful, when invention fails,
To scratch your head, and bite your nails
Jonathan Swift

In the novel, the characters can do nothing but *live*. If they keep on being good, according to pattern, or bad, according to pattern, or even volatile, according to pattern, they cease to live, and the novel falls dead. A character in a novel has got to live, or it is nothing.
D.H. Lawrence

The first thing you have to consider when writing a novel is your story, and then your story – and then your story!
Ford Madox Ford

Ernest Hemingway

If a writer stops observing he is finished. But he does not have to observe consciously nor think how it will be useful. Perhaps that would be true at the beginning. But later everything he sees goes into the great reserve of things he knows or has seen. If it is any use to know it, I always try to write on the principle of the iceberg. There is seven-eighths of it underwater for every part that shows. Anything you know you can eliminate and it only strengthens your iceberg. It is the part that doesn't show. If a writer omits something because he does not know it then there is a hole in the story.

The Old Man and the Sea could have been over a thousand pages long and had every character in the village in it and all the processes of how they made their living, were born, educated, bore children, et cetera. That is done excellently and well by other writers. In writing you are limited by what has already been done satisfactorily. So I have tried to learn to do something else. First I have tried to eliminate everything unnecessary to conveying experience to the reader so that after he or she has read something it will become a part of his or her experience and seem actually to have happened. This is very hard to do and I've worked at it very hard.

Anyway, to skip how it is done, I had unbelievable luck this time and could convey the experience completely and have it be one that no one had ever conveyed. The luck was that I had a good man and a good boy and lately writers have forgotten there still are such things. Then the ocean is worth writing about just as man is. So I was lucky there. I've seen the marlin mate and know about that. So I leave that out. I've seen a school (or pod) of more than fifty sperm whales in that same stretch of water and once harpooned one nearly sixty feet in length and lost him. So I left that out. All the stories I know from the fishing village I leave out. But the knowledge is what makes the underwater part of the iceberg.

The sincere endeavour to accomplish that creative task, to go as far on that road as his strength will carry him, to go undeterred by faltering, weariness or reproach, is the only valid justification for the worker in prose. And if his conscience is clear, his answer to those who in the fulness of a wisdom which looks for immediate profit, demand specifically to be edified, consoled, amused; who demand to be promptly improved, or encouraged, or frightened, or shocked, or charmed, must run thus: – My task which I am trying to achieve is, by the power of the written word to make you hear, to make you feel – it is, before all, to make you see. That – and no more, and it is everything. If I succeed, you shall find there according to your deserts: encouragement, consolation, fear, charm – all you demand – and, perhaps, also that glimpse of truth for which you have forgotten to ask.

Joseph Conrad

Raymond Chandler

Notes on the detective story

1 .... It must be credibly motivated, both as to the original situation
and denouement; it must consist of the plausible actions
of plausible people in plausible circumstances, it being
remembered that plausibility is largely a matter of style. This
requirement rules out most trick endings and a great many
'closed circle' stories in which the least likely character is
forcibly made over into the criminal, without convincing
anybody. It also rules out such elaborate mises-en-scène as
Christie's *Murder in a Calais Coach*, where the whole setup for
the crime requires such a fluky set of happenings that it could
never seem real.

2 .... It must be technically sound as to the methods of murder
and detection. No fantastic poisons or improper effects
from poison such as death from nonfatal doses, etc. No
use of silencers on revolvers (they won't work) or snakes
climbing bellropes ('The Speckled Band'). Such things at
once destroy the foundation of the story. If the detective
is a trained policeman, he must act like one, and have the
mental and physical equipment that go with the job. If he
is a private investigator or amateur, he must at least know
enough about police methods not to make an ass of himself.
When a policeman is made out to be a fool, as he always was
in the Sherlock Holmes stories, this not only deprecates the
accomplishment of the detective but it makes the reader doubt
the author's knowledge of his own field. Conan Doyle and Poe
were primitives in this art and stand in relation to the best
modern writers as Giotto does to da Vinci. They did things
which are no longer permissible and exposed ignorances
that are no longer tolerated. Also, police art, itself, was
rudimentary in their time. 'The Purloined Letter' would not

fool a modern cop for four minutes. Conan Doyle showed no knowledge whatever of the organization of Scotland Yard's men. Christie commits the same stupidities in our time, but that doesn't make them right. Contrast Austin Freeman, who wrote a story about a forged fingerprint ten years before police method realized such things could be done.

3 .... It must be honest with the reader. This is always said, but the implications are not realized. Important facts not only must not be concealed, they must not be distorted by false emphasis. Unimportant facts must not be projected in such a way as to make them portentous. (This creation of red herrings and false menace out of trick camera work and mood shots is the typical Hollywood mystery picture cheat.) Inferences from the facts are the detective's stock in trade; but he should disclose enough to keep the reader's mind working. It is arguable, although not certain, that inferences arising from special knowledge (e.g., Dr Thorndyke) are a bit of a cheat, because the basic theory of all good mystery writing is that at some stage not too late in the story the reader did have the materials to solve the problem. If special scientific knowledge was necessary to interpret the facts, the reader did not have the solution unless he had the special knowledge. It may have been Austin Freeman's feeling about this that led him to the invention of the inverted detective story, in which the reader knows the solution from the beginning and takes his pleasure from watching the detective trace it out a step at a time.

4 .... It must be realistic as to character, setting, and atmosphere. It must be about real people in a real world. Very few mystery writers have any talent for character work, but that doesn't mean it is not necessary. It makes the difference between the story you reread and remember and the one you skim through and almost instantly forget. Those like Valentine Williams who say the problem overrides everything are merely trying to cover up their own inability to create character.

5 .... It must have a sound story value apart from the mystery element; i.e., the investigation itself must be an adventure worth reading.

6 .... To achieve this it must have some form of suspense, even if only intellectual. This does not mean menace and especially it does not mean that the detective must be menaced by grave personal danger. This last is a trend and like all trends will exhaust itself by overimitation. Nor need the reader be kept hanging onto the edge of his chair.

The overplotted story can be dull too; too much shock may result in numbness to shock. But there must be conflict, physical, ethical or emotional, and there must be some element of danger in the broadest sense of the word.

7 .... It must have color, lift, and a reasonable amount of dash. It takes an awful lot of technical adroitness to compensate for a dull style, although it has been done, especially in England.

8 .... It must have enough essential simplicity to be explained easily when the time comes. (This is possibly the most often violated of all the rules.) The ideal denouement is one in which everything is revealed in a flash of action. This is rare because ideas that good are always rare. The explanation need not be very short (except on the screen), and often it cannot be short; but it must be interesting in itself, it must be something the reader is anxious to hear, and not a new story with a new set of characters, dragged in to justify an overcomplicated plot. Above all the explanation must not be merely a long-winded assembling of minute circumstances which no ordinary reader could possibly be expected to remember. To make the solution dependent on this is a kind of unfairness, since here again the reader did not have the solution within his grasp, in any practical sense. To expect him to remember a thousand trivialities and from them to select that three that are decisive is as unfair as to expect him to have a profound knowledge of chemistry, metallurgy, or the mating habits of the Patagonian anteater.

9 .... It must baffle a reasonably intelligent reader. This opens up a very difficult question. Some of the best detective stories ever written (those of Austin Freeman, for example) seldom baffle an intelligent reader to the end. But the reader does not guess the complete solution and could not himself have

made a logical demonstration of it. Since readers are of many minds, some will guess a cleverly hidden murder and some will be fooled by the most transparent plot. (Could 'The Red Headed League' ever really fool a modern reader?) It is not necessary or even possible to fool to the hilt the real aficionado of mystery fiction. A mystery story that consistently did that and was honest would be unintelligible to the average fan; he simply would not know what the story was all about. But there must be some important elements of the story that elude the most penetrating reader.

10 .... The solution must seem inevitable once revealed. This is the least often emphasized element of a good mystery, but it is one of the important elements of all fiction. It is not enough merely to fool or elude or sidestep the reader; you must make him feel that he ought not to have been fooled and that the fooling was honorable.

11 .... It must not try to do everything at once. If it is a puzzle story operating in a rather cool, reasonable atmosphere, it cannot also be a violent adventure or a passionate romance. An atmosphere of terror destroys logical thinking; if the story is about the intricate psychological pressures that lead apparently ordinary people to commit murder, it cannot then switch to the cool analysis of the police investigator. The detective cannot be hero and menace at the same time; the murderer cannot be a tormented victim of circumstance and also a heavy.

12 .... It must punish the criminal in one way or another, not necessarily by operation of the law. Contrary to popular (and Johnston Office) belief, this requirement has nothing much to do with morality. It is a part of the logic of detection. If the detective fails to resolve the consequences of the crime, the story is an unresolved chord and leaves irritation behind it.

The main characters in a novel must necessarily have some kinship with the author, they come out of his body as a child comes out of the womb, then the umbilical cord is cut, and they grow into independence. The more the author knows of his own character the more he can distance himself from his invented characters and the more room they have to grow in.

Graham Greene

David Mitchell

I get my major characters to write me a letter about their formative childhood experiences, other characters, the world of the book, class, money, ambition, sex, work. Writing it in their own language is crucial, choice of words is highly revealing and is the best means of delivering information about a character. It is an antidote to writer's block, I usually get stuck because I don't know my characters well enough.

A scrupulous writer, in every sentence that he writes, will ask himself at least four questions, thus:

1 .... What am I trying to say?
2 .... What words will express it?
3 .... What image or idiom will make it clearer?
4 .... Is this image fresh enough to have an effect?

And he will probably ask himself two more:

1 .... Could I put it more shortly?
2 .... Have I said anything that is avoidably ugly?

One can often be in doubt about the effect of a word or a phrase, and one needs rules that one can rely on when instinct fails. I think the following rules will cover most cases:

1 .... Never use a metaphor, simile, or other figure of speech which you are used to seeing in print.
2 .... Never use a long word where a short one will do.
3 .... If it is possible to cut a word out, always cut it out.
4 .... Never use the passive where you can use the active.
5 .... Never use a foreign phrase, a scientific word, or a jargon word if you can think of an everyday English equivalent.
6 .... Break any of these rules sooner than say anything outright barbarous.

George Orwell

Plot is no more than footprints left in the snow after your characters have run by on their way to incredible destinations. Plot is observed after the fact rather than before. It cannot precede action. It is the chart that remains when an action is through. That is all Plot ever should be. It is human desire let run, running, and reaching a goal. It cannot be mechanical it can only be dynamic.

Ray Bradbury

Muriel Spark

I invented for my Warrender Chase a war record,
a distinguished one, in Burma, and managed to
make it really credible even although I filled in the
war bit with a very few strokes, knowing, in fact,
so little about the war in Burma. It astonished me
later to find how the readers found Warrender's war
record so convincing and full when I had said so
little – one real war veteran of Burma wrote to say
how realistic he found it – but since then I've come
to learn for myself how little one needs, in the art of
writing, to convey the lot, and how a lot of words, on
the other hand, can convey so little.

Writing, for me, is not an end in
itself but a means by which some
process, beyond my ability to
articulate, is worked through to
achieve an unconscious goal.
Alan Garner

Writing, when properly managed,
is but a different word for conversation.
Laurence Sterne

Max Frisch

I have very strong feelings but I don't like to describe them. There are other ways to show them – body language, or silence – that can be very strong. And maybe, too, one has a distrust of words; one fears that they won't be interpreted correctly. It's very difficult to describe a feeling and not to lie a little bit, to put it on a higher level or to blind yourself. So I don't trust myself to describe my feelings, but I like to show them by a piece of art. And as a reader I'm the same, I don't like it if the author tells me what I have to feel. He has to urge the reader to get a feeling of shame or of hope. So there's a lot of feeling, there's a lot of emotion, but . . . not expressed in words.

I do think that novelists should be like scientists, dissecting the cadaver.
J.G. Ballard

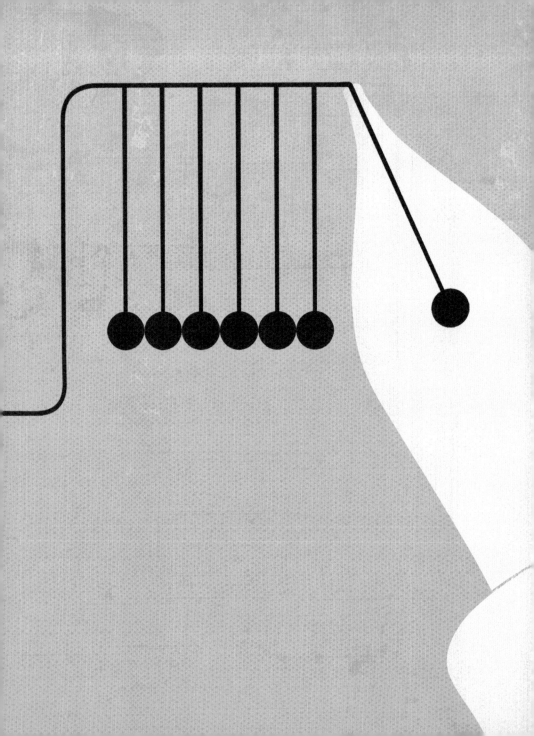

When I was 27, back in 1966, I found I
was having trouble concentrating my
attention on long narrative fiction.
For a time I experienced difficulty in
trying to read it as well as in attempting
to write it. My attention span had gone
out on me; I no longer had the patience to try to write novels.
It's an involved story, too tedious to talk about here. But I know
it has much to do now with why I write poems and short stories.
Get in, get out. Don't linger. Go on. It could be that I lost any
great ambitions at about the same time, in my late 20s. If I
did, I think it was good it happened. Ambition and a little luck
are good things for a writer to have going for him. Too much
ambition and bad luck, or no luck at all, can be killing. There
has to be talent.

Some writers have a bunch of talent; I don't know any
writers who are without it. But a unique and exact way of
looking at things, and finding the right context for expressing
that way of looking, that's something else. *The World According
to Garp* is of course the marvelous world according to John
Irving. There is another world according to Flannery
O'Connor, and others according to William Faulkner and
Ernest Hemingway. There are worlds according to Cheever,
Updike, Singer, Stanley Elkin, Ann Beattie, Cynthia Ozick,
Donald Barthelme, Mary Robison, William Kittredge, Barry
Hannah. Every great, or even every very good writer, makes
the world over according to his own specifications.

It's akin to style, what I'm talking about, but it isn't style
alone. It is the writer's particular and unmistakable signature
on everything he writes. It is his world and no other. This is
one of the things that distinguishes one writer from another.
Not talent. There's plenty of that around. But a writer who has
some special way of looking at things and who gives artistic
expression to that way of looking: that writer may be around
for a time.

Isak Dinesen said that she wrote a little every day, without
hope and without despair. Someday I'll put that on a three-

by-five card and tape it to the wall beside my desk. I have some three-by-five cards on the wall now. 'Fundamental accuracy of statement is the ONE sole morality of writing.' Ezra Pound. It is not everything by ANY means, but if a writer has 'fundamental accuracy of statement' going for him, he's at least on the right track.

I have a three-by-five up there with this fragment of a sentence from a story by Chekhov: '. . . and suddenly everything became clear to him'. I find these words filled with wonder and possibility. I love their simple clarity, and the hint of revelation that is implied. There is a bit of mystery, too. What has been unclear before? Why is it just now becoming clear? What's happened? Most of all – what now? There are consequences as a result of such sudden awakenings. I feel a sharp sense of relief – and anticipation.

I overheard the writer Geoffrey Wolff say 'No cheap tricks' to a group of writing students. That should go on a three-by-five card. I'd amend it a little to 'No tricks.' Period. I hate tricks. At the first sign of a trick or a gimmick in a piece of fiction, a cheap trick or even an elaborate trick, I tend to look for cover. Tricks are ultimately boring, and I get bored easily, which may go along with my not having much of an attention span. But extremely clever chi-chi writing, or just plain tomfoolery writing, puts me to sleep. Writers don't need tricks or gimmicks or even necessarily need to be the smartest fellows on the block. At the risk of appearing foolish, a writer sometimes needs to be able to just stand and gape at this or that thing – a sunset or an old shoe – in absolute and simple amazement. . . .

It's possible, in a poem or a short story, to write about commonplace things and objects using commonplace but precise language, and to endow those things – a chair, a window curtain, a fork, a stone, a woman's earrings – with immense, even startling power. It is possible to write a line of seemingly innocuous dialogue and have it send a chill along the reader's spine – the source of artistic delight, as Nabokov would have it. That's the kind of writing that most interests me. I hate sloppy or haphazard writing whether it flies under the banner of experimentation or else is just clumsily rendered realism. In Isaac Babel's wonderful short story, 'Guy de Maupassant', the narrator has this to say about the writing of fiction: 'No iron can pierce the heart with such force as a period put just at the right place.' This too ought to go on a three-by-five.

Evan Connell said once that he knew he was finished with a short story when he found himself going through it and taking out commas and then going through the story again and putting commas back in the same places. I like that way of working on something. I respect that kind of care for what is being done. That's all we have, finally, the words, and they had better be the right ones, with the punctuation in the right places so that they can best say what they are meant to say. If the words are heavy with the writer's own unbridled emotions, or if they are imprecise and inaccurate for some other reason – if the words are in any way blurred – the reader's eyes will slide right over them and nothing will be achieved. The reader's own artistic sense will simply not be engaged. Henry James called this sort of hapless writing 'weak specification'. . . .

I once sat down to write what turned out to be a pretty good story, though only the first sentence of the story had offered itself to me when I began it. For several days I'd been going around with this sentence in my head: 'He was running the vacuum cleaner when the telephone rang.' I knew a story was there and that it wanted telling. I felt it in my bones, that a story belonged with that beginning, if I could just have the time to write it. I found the time, an entire day – twelve, fifteen hours even – if I wanted to make use of it. I did, and I sat down in the morning and wrote the first sentence, and other sentences promptly began to attach themselves. I made the story just as I'd make a poem; one line and then the next, and the next. Pretty soon I could see a story, and I knew it was my story, the one I'd been wanting to write.

Terry Pratchett

World building is an integral part of a lot of fantasy, and this applies even in a world that is superficially our own – apart from the fact that Nelson's fleet at Trafalgar consisted of hydrogen-filled airships. It is said that, during the fantasy boom of the late eighties, publishers would maybe get a box containing two or three runic alphabets, four maps of the major areas covered by the sweep of the narrative, a pronunciation guide to the names of the main characters and, at the bottom of the box, the manuscript. Please . . . there is no need to go that far.

There is a term that readers have been known to apply to fantasy that is sometimes an unquestioning echo of better work gone before, with a static society, conveniently ugly 'bad' races, magic that works like electricity, and horses that work like cars. It's EFP, or Extruded Fantasy Product. It can be recognized by the fact that you can't tell it apart from all the other EFP.

Do not write it, and try not to read it. Read widely outside the genre. Read about the Old West (a fantasy in itself) or Georgian London or how Nelson's navy was victualled or the history of alchemy or clock making or the mail coach system. Read with the mind-set of a carpenter looking at trees.

Apply logic in places where it wasn't intended to exist. If assured that the Queen of the Fairies has a necklace made of broken promises, ask yourself what it looks like. If there is magic, where does it come from? Why isn't everyone using it? What rules will you have to give it to allow some tension in your story? How does society operate? Where does the food come from? You need to know how your world works.

G.K. Chesterton summed up fantasy as the art of taking that which is humdrum and everyday (and therefore unseen) and picking it up and showing it to us from an unfamiliar direction, so that we see it anew, with fresh eyes . . . the genre offers all the palettes of the other genres, and new colors besides. They should be used with care. It only takes a tweak to make the whole world new.

It has always been my goal to make literature out of ordinary people's lives. I don't like the extremes; I don't think that they teach us much about ourselves. And very often extreme or willfully original stories are just trying to make up for a lack of empathy on the part of the author. Writers can learn from painters. No great painter would ever choose an original subject for his paintings. Cézanne, for example, needed only a few apples and some old pots and jugs to prove his artistry. Peter Stamm

I joke a lot about nearly killing myself [when I wrote *Half of a Yellow Sun*], but it really was very intense. I think I went out of my way to read everything that I could find that was published on this period of Nigerian history. I asked tons of questions of everybody: my parents, my relatives, friends of relatives. It became really difficult to turn all of that into fiction because I had huge files of research. I found things that were so exciting, I thought, 'I didn't know the French government did that, it has to go into the book!' But then the problem was to find a way to use all of that and still make it a novel. The first draft was a disaster because it was just about how much research I had done and what I had found out. In the end the lesson was about discipline and saying to myself that it needs to be about the characters, because I realized in the first draft what was happening was the events were driving the narrative. I just thought, 'No, it's not working. It has to be the characters driving the narrative.' All those things I found out, I had to keep them in my head.

Chimamanda Ngozi Adichie

Charlotte Brontë

When authors write best, or at least,
when they write most fluently, an influence
seems to waken in them, which becomes
their master – which will have it own way –
putting out of view all behests but its own,
dictating certain words, and insisting on
their being used whether vehement or
measure in their nature; new-moulding
characters, giving unthought of turns to
incidents, rejecting carefully-elaborated
old ideas, and suddenly creating and
adopting new ones.

William Faulkner

At one time I thought the most important thing was talent. I think now that – that the young man or the young woman must possess or teach himself, train himself, in infinite patience, which is to – to try and to try and to try until it comes right. He must train himself in ruthless intolerance. That is, to throw away anything that is false no matter how much he might love that page or that paragraph. The most important thing is insight, that is . . . to wonder, to mull, to muse – to muse why it is that man does what he does. And if you have that, then I don't think the talent makes much difference, whether you've got that or not.

8 Essential Attributes of the Short Story
(and one way it differs from the novel)

1 .... There should be a clean clear surface
with much disturbance below

2 .... An anagogical level

3 .... Sentences that can stand strikingly alone

4 .... An animal within to give its blessing

5 .... Interior voices which are or become wildly
erratically exterior

6 .... Control throughout is absolutely necessary

7 .... The story's effect should transcend the
naturalness and accessibility of its situation
and language

8 .... A certain coldness is required in execution.
It is not a form that gives itself to consolation
but if consolation is offered it should come
from an unexpected quarter.

A novel wants to befriend you, a short story
almost never.

Joy Williams

Five Principal Elements

1 .... The patterns of the language – the sounds of words.

2 .... The patterns of syntax and grammar; the way the words and sentences connect themselves together; the ways their connections interconnect to form the larger units (paragraphs, sections, chapters); hence the movement of the work, its tempo, pace, gait, and shape in time.

3 .... The patterns of the images: what the words make us or let us see with the mind's eye or sense imaginatively.

4 .... The patterns of the ideas: what the words and the narration of events make us understand, or use our understanding upon.

5 .... The patterns of the feelings: what the words and the narration, by using all the above means, make us experience emotionally or spiritually, in areas of our being not directly accessible to or expressible in words.

Ursula K. Le Guin

Karl Ove Knausgaard

For several years I had tried to write about my father, but got nowhere, probably because the subject was too close to my life, and thus not easy to force into another form, which of course is a prerequisuit for literature. That is its sole law: everything has to submit to form. If any of literature's other elements are stronger than form, such as style, plot, theme, if any of these take control over form, the result is poor. That is why writers with a strong style often write poor books. That is also why writers with strong themes so often write poor books. Strong themes and styles have to be broken down before literature can come into being. It is this breaking down that is called 'writing'. Writing is more about destroying than creating.

In the broadest possible sense, writing well means to communicate clearly and interestingly and in a way that feels alive to the reader. Where there's some kind of relationship between the writer and the reader – even though it's mediated by a kind of text – there's an electricity about it. . . . In my experience with students – talented students of writing – the most important thing for them to remember is that someone who is not them and cannot read their mind is going to have to read this. In order to write effectively, you don't pretend it's a letter to some individual you know, but you never forget that what you're engaged in is a communication to another human being. The bromide associated with this is that the reader cannot read your mind. The reader cannot read your mind. That would be the biggest one.

Probably the second biggest one is learning to pay attention in different ways. Not just reading a lot, but paying attention to the way the sentences are put together, the clauses are joined, the way the sentences go to make up a paragraph . . .
David Foster Wallace

You know that fiction, prose rather, is possibly the roughest trade of all in writing. You do not have the reference, the old important reference. You have the sheet of blank paper, the pencil, and the obligation to invent truer than things can be true. You have to take what is not palpable and make it completely palpable and also have it seem normal and so that it can become a part of experience of the person who reads it.
Ernest Hemingway

A page is well written when the labour and pleasure of truthful narration supplant any other concern, including a concern with formal elegance. I belong to the category of writers who throw out the final draft and keep the rough when this practice ensures a higher degree of authenticity.

Elena Ferrante

Andre Dubus III

Habits of writing can be learned. We can to choose concrete language over overly abstract language. We can learn to use active verbs instead of passive verbs. To bring in at least three of the five senses to activate a scene. All these things we can be taught, or learn on our own from reading. These are all part of your toolbox – but that toolbox will always remain locked if the writer *is not genuinely curious about what he or she is writing about.*

A SENSE OF AN ENDING

Drawing conclusions

You'll probably be tired but equally this is the most thrilling part of writing a novel. Hopefully your plot has now defined a course of inevitability and gathered a critical mass. Your characters should be doing the things they must do, and the whole situation will be helping to carry itself . . . try not to let this very good situation lead you into a final pitfall. Don't allow yourself to be swept along into a hurried conclusion. Keep your head and give it the time and space it needs. A little discipline here will save you a lot of rewriting.

A.L. Kennedy

Conclusions are the weak
points of most authors . . .
some of the fault lies in the
very nature of a conclusion,
George Eliot   which is at best a negation.

I don't like novels that end happily. They depress me so much.
Oscar Wilde

Finishing a book is just like you took
a child out in the yard and shot it.
Truman Capote

J.M.G. Le Clézio   I have two secret ambitions. One of them is
to write, one day, a novel of such a kind that
if the hero dies in the last chapter – or, at a
pinch, develops Parkinson's disease – I shall
be swamped beneath a flood of scurrilous
anonymous letters.

The book dies a real death for me when
I write the last word. I have a little sorrow
and then I go on to the next book which is
alive. The rows of books on the shelf are to
me like very well embalmed corpses. They
are neither alive nor mine. I have no sorrow
for them because I have forgotten them,
forgotten them in its truest sense.

John Steinbeck

Arthur Conan Doyle

It was still the Sherlock Holmes stories for which the public clamoured, and these from time to time I endeavoured to supply. At last, after I had done two series of them I saw that I was in danger of having my hand forced, and of being entirely identified with what I regarded as a lower stratum of literary achievement. Therefore as a sign of my resolution I determined to end the life of my hero. The idea was in my mind when I went with my wife for a short holiday in Switzerland, in the course of which we saw there the wonderful falls of Reichenbach, a terrible place, and one that I thought would make a worthy tomb for poor Sherlock, even if I buried my banking account along with him. So there I laid him, fully determined that he should stay there – as indeed for some years he did. I was amazed at the concern expressed by the public. They say that a man is never properly appreciated until he is dead, and the general protest against my summary execution of Holmes taught me how many and how numerous were his friends. 'You Brute' was the beginning of the letter of remonstrance which one lady sent me, and I expect she spoke for others besides herself. I heard of many who wept. I fear I was utterly callous myself, and only glad to have a chance of opening out into new fields of imagination, for the temptation of high prices made it difficult to get one's thoughts away from Holmes.

. . . I do not wish to be ungrateful to Holmes, who has been a good friend to me in many ways. If I have sometimes been inclined to weary of him it is because his character admits of no light or shade. He is a calculating machine, and anything you add to that simply weakens the effect. Thus the variety of the stories must depend upon the romance and compact handling of the plots. I would say a word for Watson also, who in the course of seven volumes never shows one gleam of humour or makes one single joke. To make a real character one must sacrifice everything to consistency and remember Goldsmith's criticism of Johnson that 'he would make the little fishes talk like whales'.

For many years I suffered from a severe and continuous nervous breakdown tending to melancholia – and beyond. During about the third year of this trouble I went, in devout faith and some faint stir of hope, to a noted specialist in nervous diseases, the best known in the country. This wise man put me to bed and applied the rest cure, to which a still-good physique responded so promptly that he concluded there was nothing much the matter with me, and sent me home with solemn advice to 'live as domestic a life as far as possible', to 'have but two hours' intellectual life a day', and 'never to touch pen, brush, or pencil again' as long as I lived. This was in 1887.

I went home and obeyed those directions for some three months, and came so near the borderline of utter mental ruin that I could see over.

Then, using the remnants of intelligence that remained, and helped by a wise friend, I cast the noted specialist's advice to the winds and went to work again – work, the normal life of every human being; work, in which is joy and growth and service, without which one is a pauper and a parasite – ultimately recovering some measure of power.

Being naturally moved to rejoicing by this narrow escape, I wrote *The Yellow Wallpaper*, with its embellishments and additions, to carry out the ideal (I never had hallucinations or objections to my mural decorations) and sent a copy to the physician who so nearly drove me mad. He never acknowledged it.

The little book is valued by alienists and as a good specimen of one kind of literature. It has, to my knowledge, saved one woman from a similar fate – so terrifying her family that they let her out into normal activity and she recovered.

But the best result is this. Many years later I was told that the great specialist had admitted to friends of his that he had altered his treatment of neurasthenia since reading *The Yellow Wallpaper*.

It was not intended to drive people crazy, but to save people from being driven crazy, and it worked.

Charlotte Perkins Gilman

E.M. Forster

In the losing battle that the plot fights with the characters, it often takes a cowardly revenge. Nearly all novels are feeble at the end. This is because the plot requires to be wound up. Why is this necessary? Why is there not a convention which allows a novelist to stop as soon as he feels muddled or bored? Alas, he has to round things off, and usually the characters go dead while he is at work, and our final impression of them is through deadness.

Henning Mankell

After *The White Lioness*, I realized that the Wallander phenomenon was something I could exploit to make the most of what I had to say. At the same time I also realized that I needed to be afraid of the character I had created.

From now on there would always be a danger of my forgetting to write my novels to be performed by a full orchestra, and instead to concentrate on his horn solos. What I always needed to bear in mind was: the story is the most important thing. Always. And then to ask myself if Wallander would be a suitable solo instrument to enhance this particular story, or not.

Over and over again I would tell myself: now I'm going to do something different. I wrote texts in which he didn't appear – novels that were not about crimes, plays for the theater. Then I could return to him, drop him, write something different, then return to him again.

All the time I could hear a voice deep down inside me saying: 'You must make sure that you drop him at the right moment.' I was well aware that one day I might pick up Wallander, stare hard at him and ask myself: 'What can I think of for him to do now?' A point when he rather than the story was the most important ingredient. That would be the time to drop him. I think I can say in all honesty that Wallander has never been more important than the actual story.

Wallander never became a burden.

But there was also another warning alarm ticking away inside me. I must avoid starting to write as a sort of routine. If I did that, I would have been caught in a dangerous trap. It would be showing insufficient respect for both my readers and myself. If that happened, readers would pay good money for a book and soon discover that the author had grown tired and was simply going through the motions. As far as I was concerned, my writing would have been transformed into something to which I was no longer fully committed.

And so I stopped while it was still fun. The decision to write my last book about Wallander crept up on me slowly. It was a few years before I was ready to write the final full stop.

It was actually my wife Eva who wrote that final full stop. I had written the last word, and I asked her to press the 'full stop' key. She did so, and the story was finished.

And what now afterwards? When I am working on totally different books? I am often asked if I miss Wallander. I answer truthfully. 'I'm not the one who will miss him. It's the reader.'

I never think about Wallander. For me he is somebody who exists in my head. The three actors who have played him on the television and in the films have portrayed their own highly individual versions in brilliant fashion. It has been a great joy to me.

But I don't miss him. And I didn't repeat the mistake made by Sir Arthur Conan Doyle, who half-heartedly killed off Mr Holmes. That last Sherlock Holmes story is one of the least successful. Presumably because deep down, Doyle was doing something that he knew he would regret.

. . . In any case my story about Kurt Wallander has now come to an end. Wallander will soon retire and cease to be a police officer. He will wander around in his twilight land with his black dog Jussi. How much longer he will remain in the land of the living, I have no idea. That is presumably something he will decide for himself.

Why is an unhappy ending considered more artistic than a happy ending? . . . In some ways the unhappy ending pleases the novelist. He has set out on a voyage and announced, I have failed and must set out again. If you create a happy ending, there is a somewhat false sense of having solved life's problems.
John Fowles

Endless tweaking is not a sign of insecurity: often it is a perfectionist tendency or a desire to play, both of which are essential for a writer. The problem is not knowing when to stop and move on to the next sentence, the next paragraph, the next scene or the next chapter. Or even the next book. Therefore it is worth having a rule that says when the same comma disappears and reappears three times, it is time to move on. Or have a deadline when play must stop. If neither of those works, you will need to get someone to walk in and take your manuscript/typescript/computer away from you.

Romesh Gunesekera

I felt after I finished *Slaughterhouse-Five* that I didn't have to write at all anymore if I didn't want to. It was the end of some sort of career. I don't know why, exactly. I suppose that flowers when they're through blooming, have some sort of awareness of some purpose having been served. Flowers didn't ask to be flowers and I didn't ask to be me. At the end of *Slaughterhouse-Five*, I had the feeling that I had produced this blossom. So I had a shutting-off feeling, you know, that I had done what I was supposed to do and everything was OK. And that was the end of it. I could figure out my missions for myself after that.

Kurt Vonnegut

The last words of the nameless book were written 10 minutes ago, quite calmly too. 900 pages: L. says 200,000 words. Lord God what an amount of re-writing that means! But also, how heavenly to have brought the pen to a stop at the last line, even if most of the lines have now to be rubbed out. Anyhow the design is there. And it has taken a little less than 2 years: some months less indeed, as *Flush* intervened; therefore it has been written at a greater gallop than any of my books. The representational part accounts for the fluency. And I should say – but do I always say this? – with greater excitement: not, I think, of the same kind quite. For I have been more general, less personal. No 'beautiful writing'; much easier dialogue; but a great strain, because so many more faculties had to keep going at once, though none so pressed upon. No tears and exaltation at the end; but peace and breadth, I hope. Anyhow, if I die tomorrow, the line is there.

Virginia Woolf

Sources

p. 4 Louisa May Alcott, *Little Women* (London, Scholastic Books, 2014).

BECOMING A WRITER

p. 10 Jack Kerouac, 'Are Writers Made or Born?', *Writer's Digest* (1962), in *The Portable Jack Kerouac* (London, Penguin, 1996).

D.H. Lawrence, 'Why the Novel Matters', *Phoenix: the Posthumous Papers of D.H. Lawrence, 1936*, edited by Edward D. McDonald (New York, Viking Press, 1936).

p. 11 Mark Twain, 'A General Reply', *Galaxy* (November 1870).

p. 12 James Baldwin, interview with Jack Gould, *New York Times* (31 May 1964).

p. 13 Jean Paul Sartre, *Words*, translated by Irene Clephane (London, Penguin, 2000).

p. 14 Zora Neale Hurston, *I Love Myself When I am Laughing* (New York, The Feminist Press, 1979).

Henry David Thoreau, *Men of Concord and some others as portrayed in the Journal of Henry David Thoreau*, edited by Francis H. Allen (Boston, Houghton Mifflin Co., 1936)

p. 15 Joan Didion, 'On Keeping a Notebook', *Slouching Towards Bethlehem* (London, André Deutsch, 1969).

p. 17 Colette, *Earthly Paradise: Colette's Autobiography Drawn from the Writings of her Lifetime by Robert Phelps*, translated by Helen Beauclerk *et al.* (London, Sphere, 1970).

p. 18 George Orwell, 'Why I Write?', *Gangrel* (Summer 1946), reprinted in *The Collected Essays, Journalism and Letters of George Orwell, Volume 4: In Front of Your Nose 1945–1950* (Penguin, London, 1970).

p. 22 Jhumpa Lahiri, 'Trading Stories: Notes from an Apprenticeship', *New Yorker, Reflections* (June 13 & 20, 2011).

Ian McEwan, *Another Round at the Pillars: Essays, Poems and Reflections on Ian Hamilton*, edited by David Harsent (London, Faber & Faber, 1999).

p. 23 Mary Shelley, 'Introduction', *Frankenstein or, The Modern Prometheus* (1831 edition), edited with an introduction by M.K. Joseph (Oxford University Press, 1969).

Anais Nin, *The Diary of Anais Nin, Volume 5: 1947–1955*, edited by Gunther Stuhlmann (San Diego, New York, London, Harcourt Brace Jovanvich, 1975).

p. 25 Hanif Kureishi, *Dreaming and Becoming: Reflections on Writing and Politics* (London, Faber & Faber, 2002).

p. 26 F. Scott Fitzgerald, 'Who's Who and Why', *Saturday Evening Post* (18 September 1920).

p. 30 T.H. White, *England Have My Bones* (London, Macdonald Futura, 1981).

Thomas Mann, *Essays of Three Decades*, translated by H.T. Lowe-Porter (London, Secker & Warburg, 1935).

p. 31 Jean Rhys, 'The Art of Fiction 64', interview with Elizabeth Vreeland, *Paris Review 76* (Fall 1979).

p. 32 Margaret Atwood, *Negotiating with the Dead: A Writer on Writing* (London, Virago, 2003).

p. 34 Emily Dickinson (attrib.), quoted in *The Crucible of Language: How Language and Mind Create Meaning*, by Vyvyan Evans (Cambridge University Press, 2015).

Samuel Johnson, *Rambler 3* (27 March 1750), reprinted in *The Works of Samuel Johnson, Volume 1* (New York, George Dearborn, 1837).

p. 35 Gabriel García Márquez, 'The Art of Fiction 69', interview with Peter H. Stone, *Paris Review 82* (Winter 1981).

Renata Adler, *Toward a Radical Middle* (New York, Random House, 1969).

p. 36 Stephen King, *On Writing: a memoir of the craft* (London, Hodder & Stoughton, 2000).

p. 37 J.G. Ballard, 'An Investigative Spirit: Travis Elborough talks to J.G. Ballard', in *Empire of the Sun* (London, Harper Perennial, 2008).

p. 39 Chimamanda Ngozi Adichie, interview with John Zuarino, *Bookslut* (August 2009): http://www.bookslut.com/features/2009 _ 08 _ 014928.php

p. 40 Orhan Pamuk, 'The Art of Fiction 187', interview with Ángel Gurría-Quintana, *Paris Review 175* (Fall/Winter, 2005).

David Foster Wallace, *Quack This Way: David Foster Wallace & Bryan A. Garner Talk Language and Writing* (Dallas, RosePen Books, 2013).

p. 41 David Mitchell, 'Advice to a Young Writer: Brilliantly Bad Originality is Better Than Competent Mimicry', speaking to Irina Rey at the University of Pittsburgh's Writing Program at Literary Hub (18 November 2015): http://lithub.com/david-mitchells-writing-advice

p. 42 Jenny Erpenbeck, 'Five Questions for Jenny Erpenbeck', *Haaretz* (17 February 2011): http://www.haaretz.com/life/books/five-questions-for-jenny-erpenbeck-1.344042

p. 43 R.L. Stine, interview with Zachary Petit in *2014 Children's Writer's & Illustrator's Market* (Writer's Digest Books, 2013).

Hilary Mantel, quoted in A*gony and the Ego: The Art and Strategy of Fiction Writing Explained*, edited by Clare Boylan (London, Penguin, 1993).

p. 45 J.K. Rowling, from author's website: http://www.jkrowling.com/textonly/en/biography.cfm

p. 46 Haruki Murakami, W*hat I Talk About When I Talk About Running: A Memoir*, translated by Philip Gabriel (London, Vintage, 2009).

p. 47 James Salter, 'Some for Glory, Some for Praise', National Endowment for the Arts website: https://www.arts.gov/operation-homecoming/essays-writing/some-glory-some-praise

Lorrie Moore, 'How to Become a Writer, or Have You Earned This Cliche?', *New York Times* (3 March 1985).

p. 48 Tom Perrotta, 'Travis Elborough talks to Tom Perrotta', in *The Abstinence Teacher* (London, Harper Perennial, 2008).

Ray Bradbury, in *The Legends of Literature: Essays from Writer's Digest Magazine*, edited by Philip Sexton (Cincinnati, Ohio, Writer's Digest, 2007).

p. 49 Julian Barnes, *Flaubert's Parrot* (London, Cape, 1984).

Deborah Levy, *Things I don't want to know: a response to George Orwell's 1946 essay 'Why I Write'* (London, Notting Hill Editions, 2013).

METHOD AND MEANS

p. 52 Anthony Trollope, *An Autobiography*, edited by H.M. Trollop (Edinburgh, London, W. Blackwood & Sons, 1883).

p. 53 Leo Tolstoy, *Talks with Tolstoi*, translated by S.S. Koteliansky and Virginia Woolf (Richmond, Hogarth Press, 1923).

Thomas Hardy, from a letter in December 1883 to a Mr A.A. Reade, in *The Early Life of Thomas Hardy, 1840–1891*, by Florence Emily Hardy (London, Macmillan, 1928).

p. 54 Walter Scott, 'Introductory Epistle' to *The Fortunes of Nigel: A Romance* (Edinburgh, Archibald Constable & Co.; London, Hurst, Robinson, & Co., 1822).

p. 56 Henry David Thoreau, *The Heart of Thoreau's Journals*, edited by Odell Shepard (Boston, New York, Houghton Mifflin Co., 1927).

p. 58 Kate Chopin, 'My Writing Method', *Post-Depatch* (St Louis, 1899).

p. 59 Jodi Picoult, 'Frequently Asked Questions': http://www.jodipicoult.com/faqs.html (August 2016).

p. 60 Arnold Bennett, *The Journals of Arnold Bennett*, edited by Newman Flower (London, Cassell & Co. Ltd., 1932).

Jack London, 'Getting into Print', *The Editor* (March 1903).

Sources

p. 61 H.P. Lovecraft, letter to Lillian D. Clark (1 September 1925), in *Selected Letters II (1925–1929)*, edited by August Derleth and Donald Wandrei (Sauk City, WI, Arkham House Publishers, Inc., 1968).

Katherine Mansfield, *Journal of Katherine Mansfield*, edited by John Middleton Murry (London, Constable, 1927).

p. 62 John Boyne, 'My Writing Day', *Guardian* (n.d.)

James Joyce, *Conversations with James Joyce/ Arthur Power*, edited by Clive Hart Arthur Power (London, Millington, 1974).

p. 63 Ernest Hemingway, 'Monologue to the Maestro: A High Seas Letter', in *Esquire* (October 1935).

p. 65 Ford Madox Ford, 'Introduction' to *It Was a Nightingale* (London, William Heinemann, 1934).

p. 66 C.S. Lewis, *Surprised by Joy: The Shape of My Early Life* (London, Collins, 1959).

p. 67 Stephen King, *On Writing: a memoir of the craft* (London, Hodder & Stoughton, 2000).

p. 68 E.L. Doctorow, 'The Myth Maker', interview with Bruce Weber, *The New York Times* (20 October 1985).

Helle Helle, 'An Interview with Helle Helle', interview with Cara Benson, *Bookslut* (January 2016): http://www.bookslut.com/features/2016 _ 01 _ 021333.php

p. 69 Flannery O Connor, 'The Regional Writer', in *Esprit* (Winter 1963).

p. 70 Jack Kerouac, 'Belief & Technique for Modern Prose: List of Essentials', in *Evergreen Review* (Spring 1959).

p. 72 H.G. Wells, interview in *To-Day* (11 September 1897) reprinted in *Writers on Writing*, edited by Walter Ernest Allen (London, Phoenix House, 1948).

p. 74 Roald Dahl, interview with Todd McCormack (1988): https://www.roalddahl.com/create-and-learn/write/roald-dahl-on-writing

p. 75 Muriel Spark, *A Far Cry From Kensington* (London, Constable, 1988).

Georges Simenon, 'The Art of Fiction 9', interview with Carvel Collins, *Paris Review 9* (Summer 1955).

p. 76 Joyce Carole Oates, 'Letter to a Fiction Writer', *The Ontario Review* (1999).

p. 77 Fay Weldon, in *The Writer's Imagination: Interviews with Major International Women Novelists*, by Olga Kenyon (Bradford, University of Bradford Print Unit, 1992).

p. 78 Tom Perrotta, 'Travis Elborough talks to Tom Perrotta', in *The Abstinence Teacher* (London, Harper Perennial, 2008).

Miranda July, 'Printing', interview with Carrie Brownstein, *Interview* (21 January 2014): http://www.interviewmagazine.com/culture/miranda-july-1

p. 79 Annie Dillard, *The Writing Life* (New York, Harper Perennial, 1990).

p. 80 Isaac Asimov, 'It's An Asimovalanche! The One-man Book-a-Month Club Has Just Published His 179th', interview with Brad Darrach, *People* (22 November 1976).

p. 82 Hanif Kureishi, *Dreaming and Becoming: Reflections on Writing and Politics* (London, Faber & Faber, 2002).

p. 83 Will Self, 'Writer's Rooms', *Guardian* (6 April 2007).

Neil Gaiman, 'Where Do You Get Your Ideas?' from author's website: http://www.neilgaiman.com/Cool_Stuff/Essays/Essays_By_Neil/Where_do_you_get_your_ideas%3F

p. 84 Alan Garner, 'Alan Garner speaks to Travis Elborough', in *The Stone Book Quartet* (London, Harper Perennial, 2006).

p. 85 Zadie Smith, 'Zadie Smith's Rules for Writers', *Guardian* (22 February 2010).

p. 86 Rivka Galchen, 'Rivka Galchen speaks to Travis Elborough', in *Atmospheric Disturbances* (London, Harper Perennial, 2009).

p. 87 William Faulkner, quoted in *Advice to Writers*, by Jon Winokur (New York, Random House, 2000).

p. 88 David Foster Wallace, *Quack This Way: David Foster Wallace & Bryan A. Garner Talk Language and Writing* (Dallas, RosePen Books, 2013).

John Grisham, interview in *San Francisco Chronicle* (5 February 2008).

p. 89 Jonathan Franzen, 'Modern Life Has Become Extremely Distracting', *Guardian* (2 October 2015).

p. 91 Toby Litt, from author's blog (6 May 2016): https://tobylitt.wordpress.com/2016/05/06/sport-or-what-can-writers-learn-from-athletes-and-coaches

p. 92 Richard Ford, in 'Ten Rules for Writing Fiction, *Guardian* (20 February 2010): https://www.theguardian.com/books/2010/feb/20/ten-rules-for-writing-fiction-part-one

p. 93 Emma Tennant, quoted in *Delighting the Heart: A Notebook for Women Writers*, edited by Susan Sellers (Women's Press, 1989).

John Keats, *The Letters of John Keats*, edited by M.B. Forman (Oxford University Press, 1935).

p. 94 David Mitchell, 'Neglect Everything Else', *The Atlantic* (23 September 2014): https://www.theatlantic.com/entertainment/archive/2014/09/the-simple-profound-act-of-perceiving-the-world/380659

p. 96 Roberto Bolaño, *Between Parentheses: Essays, Articles and Speeches, 1998–2003*, edited by Ignacio Echevarria, translated by Natasha Wimmer (New York, New Directions, 2011).

p. 98 Hilary Mantel, 'Growing a Book', *Writer Diaries* (17 August 2014): http://writerdiaries.com/hilary-mantel-art-growing-book

p. 100 Annie Dillard, *The Writing Life* (New York, Harper Perennial, 1990).

J.G. Ballard, 'PS Section' by Travis Elborough, *Millennium People* (London, Harper Perennial, 2003).

p. 101 Paul Beatty, 'My Writing Day', *Guardian* (29 October 2016).

p. 102 Haruki Murakami, *What I Talk About When I Talk About Running: A Memoir*, translated by Philip Gabriel (London, Vintage, 2009).

p. 103 Philip Roth, 'The Art of Fiction 84', interview with Hermione Lee, *Paris Review 93* (Fall 1984).

p. 105 John Steinbeck, *Steinbeck: A Life in Letters*, edited by Elaine Steinbeck and Robert Wallsten (London, Penguin, 2001).

p. 106 F. Scott Fitzgerald, letter to Max Perkins (11 March 1935), in *The Letters of F. Scott Fitzgerald*, edited by Andrew Turnbull (London, Bodley Head, 1964).

p. 107 Amy Tan, quoted in *The Secret Miracle: The Novelist's Handbook*, edited by Daniel Alarcon (New York, Henry Holt, 2010).

Katherine Mansfield, *The Collected Letters of Katherine Mansfield: Volume IV: 1920-1921*, edited by Vincent O'Sullivan and Margaret Scott (Oxford University Press, 2004).

p. 108 Geoff Dyer, *Out of Sheer Rage: In the Shadow of D.H. Lawrence* (London, Little, Brown, 1997).

p. 109 P.G. Wodehouse, 'In Their Own Words: British Novelists', broadcast on *Among the Ruins: 1919–1939* (BBC Radio).

FAILING

p. 112 E.M. Forster, interviewed by the BBC, *Monitor* (1959).

p. 113 Samuel Beckett, *Worstward Ho* (London, Calder, 1983).

Anthony Trollope, *An Autobiography*, edited by H.M. Trollope (Edinburgh, London, W. Blackwood & Sons, 1883).

p. 114 Eleanor Catton, interview with Elizabeth Kuruvilla, *Live Mint* (15 February 2017): http://www.livemint.com/Leisure/pzEq1u3frRLWQehmXjyzHL/Eleanor-Catton-In-the-last-year-Ive-really-struggled-with.html

Sources

p. 115 Jonathan Franzen, 'Writer's Toolbox', interview in *Gotham Writers* (undated): https://www.writingclasses.com/toolbox/author-q-a/jonathan-franzen?page=7&per-page=50

p. 117 Martin Amis, 'The Art of Fiction 151', interview with Francesca Riviere, *Paris Review 146* (Spring 1998).

p. 118 Charles Bukowski, *Sunlight Here I Am: Interviews and Encounters 1963-1993*, edited by David Stephen Calonne (Sun Dog Press, 2003).

Virginia Woolf, 'A Room of One's Own' (1929) in *Collected Essays* (London, Hogarth Press, 1966).

p. 119 Gore Vidal, interview in *Writer's Digest* (March 1975).

J.M. Coetzee, *Here and Now: Letters 2008–2011*, by Paul Auster and J.M. Coetzee (London, Faber & Faber, 2013).

p. 120 Anne Enright, 'Failure Is What We Do. It is Built In', *Guardian* (22 June 2013).

p. 121 Amy Tan, quoted in *The Secret Miracle*, edited by Daniel Alarcon (New York, Henry Holt, 2010).

p. 122 Han Kang, 'Violence and Being Human: A Conversation with Han Kang by Krys Lee', *World Literature Today* (May 2016).

Ray Bradbury, keynote address at The Sixth Annual Writer's Symposium by the Sea, quoted by *Brain Pickings* (18 May 2012): https://www.brainpickings.org/2012/05/18/commencement-speeches-2/

p. 123 Tim Winton, 'Waiting for the Wave', interview with Aida Edemariam, *Guardian* (28 June 2008).

Orhan Pamuk, 'The Art of Fiction 187', interviewed with Ángel Gurría-Quintana, *Paris Review 175* (Fall/Winter 2005).

p. 124 Philip Pullman, quoted by Emily Temple, '13 Famous Writers on Overcoming Writer's Block' *Flavorwire* (3 November 2012): http://flavorwire.com/343207/13-famous-writers-on-overcoming-writers-block/13

p. 126 Jane Austen, letter to Stanier Clarke (11 December 1815), in *Jane Austen's Letters to her sister Cassandra and others,* edited by R.W. Chapman (Oxford, Clarendon Press, 1932).

p. 127 Alice Munro, 'The Art of Fiction 137', interview with Jeanne McCulloch and Mona Simpson, *Paris Review 131* (Summer 1994).

p. 128 Angela Carter, in *The Writer's Imagination: Interviews with Major International Women Novelists*, by Olga Kenyon (Bradford, University of Bradford Print Unit, 1992).

Ring Lardner, quoted in *Writers on Writing: A Compendium of Quotations on the Writer's Art*, edited by Jon Winokur (London, Headline, 1988).

p. 129 Charles Dickens, *The Letters of Charles Dickens*, edited by Walter Dexter (London, Bloomsbury, Nonesuch Press, 1938).

p. 131 Junot Díaz, *O, The Oprah Magazine* (October 2009), quoted at http://www.junotdiaz.com/2012/05/19/the-list/

p. 133 Stephen King, *On Writing: A Memoir of the Craft* (London, Hodder & Stoughton, 2000).

Hanif Kureishi, *Dreaming and Becoming: Reflections on Writing and Politics* (London, Faber & Faber, 2002).

p. 134 Margaret Atwood, 'Get Back on the Horse that Threw You', *Guardian* (22 June 2013).

p. 135 Ursula K. Le Guin, *Dancing at the Edge of the World: Thoughts on Words, Women, Places* (London, Gollancz, 1989).

p. 136 Edith Wharton, *A Backward Glance* (New York, London, D. Appleton-Century Co., 1934).

p. 137 Joe Dunthorne, interview with Tom Seymour, *Ideas Tap* (18 July 2011): http://www.ideastap.com/IdeasMag/all-articles/Joe-Dunthorne-Writer-Interview

p. 138 Lionel Shriver, 'No One Wants to Buy a Book about Disappointment', *Guardian* (22 June 2013).

p. 141 Hilary Mantel, 'Hilary Mantel's Rules for Writers', *Guardian* (22 February 2010).

J.B. Priestley, quoted in *The Craft of Fiction*, by Will Knott (Askmar Publishing, 2002).

p. 142 Jennifer Egan, interview with Astri von Arbin Ahlander, *The Days of Yore* (19 April 2011): http://thedaysofyore.com/2011/jennifer-egan

p. 144 H.G. Wells, quoted in *The Diplomate*, Volume 19, (National Board of Medical Examiners, 1947).

Samuel Johnson, quoted in James Boswell, *The Life of Johnson* (Oxford, Clarendon Press, 1934).

p. 145 Gabriel García Márquez, 'The Art of Fiction 69', interview with Peter H. Stone, *Paris Review 82* (Winter 1981).

Orson Scott Card, interview with Tina Morgan, *Fiction Factor*: http://www.fictionfactor.com/interviews/orsonscottcard.html

p. 146 Charles Bukowski, from *The Last Night of the Earth Poems* (Harper Collins, 2009).

Maya Angelou, quoted in *The Writer's Idea Book 10th Anniversary Edition: How to Develop Great Ideas for Fiction, Nonfiction, Poetry, and Screenplays*, by Jack Heffron (Writer's Digest Books, 2012).

p. 147 George R.R. Martin, 'Not a Blog' (2 January 2016): http://grrm.livejournal.com/465247.html?thread=23480415

p. 148 Neil Gaiman, 'A Conversation With Neil Gaiman', by Claire E. White, *The Internet Writing Journal* (March 1999).

p. 150 John Banville, 'Fully Booked: Q&A with John Banville', interview with Travis Elborough in *The Sea* (London, Picador 40th Anniversary Edition, 2012).

Washington Irving, 'Memorial of Washington Irving', *The Knickerbocker: Or, New-York Monthly Magazine* (1860).

p. 151 F. Scott Fitzgerald, *Fitzgerald: My Lost City: Personal Essays, 1920–1940: Vol. 4* (Cambridge University Press, 2005).

Jorge Luis Borges, *Borges at Eighty: Conversations*, edited and with photographs by Willis Barnstone (Bloomington, Indiana University Press, 1982).

THE WRITER'S ART

p. 154 Walter Scott, *The Miscellaneous Prose Works, Volume III* (Robert Cadell, Edinburgh, 1834).

p. 155 Samuel Johnson, *Rambler 3* (27 March 1750), in *The Works of Samuel Johnson, Volume 1* (New York, George Dearborn, 1837).

Herman Melville, *Moby Dick* (William Collins, London, 2013).

p. 156 John Updike, 'Writers on Themselves', *The New York Times* (17 August 1986).

Jorge Luis Borges, *Borges at Eighty: Conversations*, edited and with photographs by Willis Barnstone (Bloomington, Indiana University Press, 1982).

p. 157 Charlotte Brontë, 'Editor's Preface to the New Edition of Wuthering Heights', *Wuthering Heights* (John Murray, London, 1910).

p. 158 Charles Dickens, letter to Jane Brookfield (20 February 1866), in *The Selected Letters of Charles Dickens*, edited by Jenny Hartley (Oxford University Press, 2012).

p. 159 Wilkie Collins, 'Preface to the Present Edition (1861)', *The Woman in White* (Richmond, Alma Classics, 2009).

p. 160 Thomas Hardy, 'The Profitable Reading of Fiction', *The Forum* (March 1888).

p. 161 George Eliot, 'Storytelling', *Essays and Leaves from a Notebook*, edited by Charles Lee Lewes (Edinburgh, Blackwood, 1884).

p. 162 Elmore Leonard, *Elmore Leonard's 10 Rules of Writing* (New York, William Morrow, 2007).

p. 164 Mark Twain, letter to D.W. Bowser (20 March 1880), *Mark Twain Project* (Mark Twain Papers, California Digital Library, UC Press, 2007–16): http://www.marktwainproject.org/xtf/view?docId=letters/UCCL01772.xml;style=letter;brand=mtp

p. 165 Leo Tolstoy, *A Calendar of Wisdom: Daily Thoughts to Nourish the Soul*, translated by Peter Sekirin (New York, Prentice Hall & IBD, 1997).

Sources

p. 166 Robert Louis Stevenson, 'Some Gentlemen in Fiction', *Scribner's* (June 1888).

p. 167 Oscar Wilde, quoted in *Oscar Wilde: The Story of an Unhappy Friendship*, by R.H. Sherard (London, Greening & Co., 1909).

Edgar Allen Poe, 'The Philosophy of Composition' *Graham's Magazine Vol. XXVIII, No.4* (April 1846).

p. 168 George Bernard Shaw, letter to *The Times* (1907), quoted in *The Story of English: How the English Language Conquered the World*, by Philip Gooden (Quercus, 2011).

William Makepeace Thackeray, *The History of Pendennis* (Lenox, Hard Press, 2006).

p. 169 Catherine Drinker Bowen, *Adventures of a Biographer* (London, Little, Brown, 1959).

Arthur Conan Doyle, *Memories and Adventures* (London, Hodder & Stoughton, 1924).

p. 170 Anton Chekhov, letter to Madame M.V. Kiselyov (14 January 1887), from *Letters on the Short Story, the Drama and Other Literary Topics*, selected and edited by Louis S. Friedland (Benjamin Blom, 1966).

F. Scott Fitzgerald, *The Crack-Up*, edited by Edmund Wilson (New York, New Directions, 1945).

p. 171 Willa Cather, 'On the Art of Fiction', *The Borzoi* (1920).

p. 173 Vladimir Nabokov, *Lectures on Literature* (New York, Harcourt Brace Jovanovich, 1981).

p. 174 H.P. Lovecraft, *Writings in the United Amateur 1915–1922* (Project Gutenberg, 2009).

p. 175 James Joyce, in *Conversations with James Joyce*, by Arthur Power (Dublin, The Lilliput Press Ltd, 2000).

Jonathan Swift, 'A Rhapsody' (1733), *The Poetical Works of Jonathan Swift* (Edinburgh, Mundell and Son, 1794).

p. 176 D.H. Lawrence, 'Why the Novel Matters', *Phoenix: the posthumous papers of D.H. Lawrence,* 1936, edited by Edward D. McDonald (New York, Viking Press, 1936).

Ford Madox Ford, *It was the Nightingale* (Manchester, Carcanet Press, 2007).

p. 177 Ernest Hemingway, 'The Art of Fiction 21', interview with by George Plimpton, *Paris Review 18* (Spring 1958).

p. 178 Joseph Conrad, *Notes on My Books* (New York, Doubleday, Page, 1921).

p. 180 Raymond Chandler, 'Twelve Notes on the Mystery Novel', *The Notebooks of Raymond Chandler*, edited by Frank MacShane (New York, The Ecco Press, 1976).

p. 184 Graham Greene, *Ways of Escape* (London, Vintage, 1999).

David Mitchell, quoted in a review by Chris Park (Northern Soul, 2014): http://www.northernsoul. me.uk/david-mitchell/

p. 185 George Orwell, *Politics and the English Language* (London, Penguin, 2013).

p. 186 Ray Bradbury, *Zen in the Art of Writing* (London, Harper Voyager, 2015).

p. 187 Muriel Spark, *Loitering with Intent* (London, Virago, 2007).

p. 188 Alan Garner, 'PS Section' by Travis Elborough, *The Stone Book Quartet* (London, Harper Perennial, 2006).

Laurence Sterne, *Tristram Shandy* (London, Wordsworth Classics, 1996).

p. 189 Max Frisch, 'The Art of Fiction 113', interview with Jodi Daynard, *Paris Review 113* (Winter II, 1989).

J.G. Ballard, quoted in 'PS Section' by Travis Elborough, *Hello America* (London, Harper Perennial, 2008).

p. 191 Raymond Carver, 'A Storyteller's Shoptalk', *New York Times* (15 February 1981).

p. 194 Terry Pratchett, *A Slip of the Keyboard: Collected Nonfiction* (London, Doubleday, 2014).

p. 195 Peter Stamm 'This Week in Fiction: Peter Stamm', interview with Deborah Treisman, *New Yorker* (2012): http://www.newyorker.com/books/page-turner/this-week-in-fiction-peter-stamm

p. 196 Chimamanda Ngozi Adichie, 'An Interview with Chimamanda Ngozi Adichie', by John Zuarino, *Bookslut* (2009): http://www.bookslut.com/features/2009 _ 08 _ 014928.php

p. 197 Charlotte Brontë, letter to G.H. Lewes (12 January 1848), in *The Life of Charlotte Brontë*, by Elizabeth Gaskell (London, Penguin Classics, 1998).

p. 198 William Faulkner, 'Faulkner at Virginia', Press Conference (20 May 1957): http://faulkner.lib.virginia.edu/display/wfaudio17

p. 200 Joy Williams, 'Joy Williams Explains How to Write a Short Story', interview with Lincoln Michel, *Vice* (2016): https://www.vice.com/en_us/article/joy-williams-ninety-nine-stories-of-god-how-to-write-a-short-story

p. 201 Ursula K. Le Guin, 'Where Do You Get Your Ideas From?' *Dancing at the Edge of the World* (New York, Grove Press, 1989).

p. 202 Karl Ove Knausgaard, *A Death in the Family: My Struggle Book 1* (London, Vintage, 2013).

p. 203 David Foster Wallace, *Quack This Way: David Foster Wallace & Bryan A. Garner Talk Language and Writing* (Dallas, RosePen Books, 2013).

p. 204 Ernest Hemingway, *Selected Letters 1917–1961* (London, Scribner Classics, 2003).

Elena Ferrante, 'Women of 2015: Elena Ferante, Writer', interview with Liz Jobey, *Financial Times* (11 December 2015).

p. 205 Andre Dubus III, 'The Case for Writing a Story Before Knowing How it Ends', interview with Joe Fassler, *The Atlantic* (2013): https://www.theatlantic.com/entertainment/archive/2013/10/the-case-for-writing-a-story-before-knowing-how-it-ends/280387/

A SENSE OF AN ENDING

p. 208 A.L. Kennedy, *Novel Writing: A Writers' & Artists' Companion*, edited by Romesh Gunesekera and A.L. Kennedy (London, Bloomsbury, 2015).

p. 209 George Eliot, *George Eliot Letters*, edited by Gordon S. Haight (New Haven, Yale University Press, 1954–5).

Oscar Wilde, *The Importance of Being Earnest* (London, Penguin Classics, 2007).

p. 210 Truman Capote (attrib.), quoted in *Writer's Digest*: http://www.writersdigest.com/writing-quotes

J.M.G. Le Clézio, *The Interrogation* (London, Penguin, 2008).

p. 211 John Steinbeck, 'The Art of Fiction 45', interview with Nathaniel Benchley *Paris Review 48* (Fall 1969).

p. 213 Arthur Conan Doyle, *Memories and Adventures* (London, Hodder & Stoughton, 1924).

p. 214 Charlotte Perkins Gilman, 'Why I Wrote The Yellow Wallpaper', in *The Forerunner* (October 1913).

p. 215 E.M. Forster, *Aspects of the Novel* (London, Penguin Classics, 2005).

p. 216 Henning Mankell, *An Event in Autumn* (London, Vintage, 2015).

p. 218 John Fowles, 'Talk with John Fowles', interview with Mel Gussow, *The New York Times* (13 November 1977).

p. 220 Romesh Gunesekera, *Novel Writing: A Writers' & Artists' Companion*, edited by Romesh Gunesekera and A.L. Kennedy (London, Bloomsbury, 2015).

p. 221 Kurt Vonnegut, *Conversations with Kurt Vonnegut*, edited by William Rodney Allen (Mississippi, University Press Mississippi, 1988).

p. 222 Virginia Woolf, *Selected Diaries* (London, Vintage, 2008).

Index of authors

Adichie, Chimamanda Ngozi (1977–) 39, 196
Adler, Renata (1937–) 35
Alcott, Louisa May (1832–88) 4
Amis, Martin (1949–) 117
Angelou, Maya (1928–2014) 146
Asimov, Isaac (1992–) 80
Atwood, Margaret (1939–) 32, 134
Austen, Jane (1775–1817) 126

Baldwin, James (1924–87) 12
Ballard, J.G. (1930–2009) 37, 100, 189
Banville, John (1945–) 150
Barnes, Julian (1946–) 49
Beatty, Paul (1962–) 101
Beckett, Samuel (1906–89) 113
Bennett, Arnold (1867–1931) 60
Bolaño, Roberto (1953–2003) 96–7
Borges, Jorge Luis (1899–1986) 151, 156
Bowen, Catherine Drinker (1897–1973) 169
Boyne, John (1971–) 62
Bradbury, Ray (1920–2012) 48, 122, 186
Brontë, Charlotte (1816–55) 157, 197
Bukowski, Charles (1920–94) 118, 146

Capote, Truman (1924–84) 210
Card, Orson Scott (1951–) 145
Carter, Angela (1940–92) 128
Carver, Raymond (1938–88) 191–3
Cather, Willa (1873–1947) 171
Catton, Eleanor (1985–) 114
Chandler, Raymond (1888–1959) 180–3

Chekhov, Anton (1860–1904) 170
Chopin, Kate (1850–1904) 58
Coetzee, J.M. (1940–) 119
Collette (1873–1954) 17
Collins, Wilkie (1824–89) 158
Conan Doyle, Arthur (1859–1930) 169, 213
Conrad, Joseph (1857–1924) 178

Dahl, Roald (1916–90) 74
Díaz, Junot (1968–) 131–2
Dickens, Charles (1812–70) 129, 158
Dickinson, Emily (1830–86) 34
Didion, Joan (1934–) 15
Dillard, Annie (1945–) 79, 100
Doctorow, E.L. (1931–2015) 68
Dubus III, Andre (1936–99) 205
Dunthorne, Joe (1982–) 137
Dyer, Geoff (1958–) 108–9

Egan, Jennifer (1962–) 142
Eliot, George (1819–80) 161, 209
Enright, Anne (1962–) 120–1
Erpenbeck, Jenny (1967–) 42

Faulkner, William (1897–1962) 87, 107, 198
Ferrante, Elena (1943–) 204
Fitzgerald, F. Scott (1896–1940) 26–9, 106, 151, 170
Ford, Ford Madox (1873–1939) 65, 176
Ford, Richard (1944–) 92
Forster, E.M. (1879–1970) 112, 215
Fowles, John (1926–2005) 218

Franzen, Jonathan (1959–) 89, 115
Frisch, Max (1911–91) 189

Gaiman, Neil (1960–) 83, 148
Galchen, Rivka (1976–) 86–7
Garner, Alan (1934–) 84, 188
Gilman, Charlotte Perkins (1860–1935) 214
Greene, Graham (1904–91) 184
Grisham, John (1955–) 88
Gunesekera, Romesh (1954–) 220

Hardy, Thomas (1840–1928) 53, 160
Helle, Helle (1965–) 68
Hemingway, Ernest (1899–1961) 63, 177, 204
Hurston, Zora Neale (1891–1960) 14

Irving, Washington (1783–1859) 150

Johnson, Samuel (1709–84) 34, 143, 155
Joyce, James (1882–1941) 62, 175
July, Miranda (1974–) 78

Kang, Han (1970–) 122
Keats, John (1795–1821) 93
Kennedy, A.L. (1965–) 208
Kerouac, Jack (1922–69) 10, 70–1
King, Stephen (1947–) 36, 67, 133
Knausgaard, Karl Ove (1968–) 202
Kureishi, Hanif (1954–) 25, 82, 133

Lahiri, Jhumpa (1967–) 22
Lardner, Ring (1885–1933) 128
Lawrence, D.H. (1885–1930)
  10, 176
Le Clézio, J.M.G. (1940–) 210
Le Guin, Ursula K. (1929–)
  135, 201
Leonard, Elmore (1925–2013)
  162
Levy, Deborah (1959–) 49
Lewis, C.S. (1898–1963)
  66–7
Litt, Toby (1968–) 91
London, Jack (1876–1916) 60
Lovecraft, H.P. (1890–1937)
  61

Mankell, Henning (1948–2015)
  216–17
Mann, Thomas (1875–1955) 30
Mansfield, Katherine (1888–1923)
  61, 107
Mantel, Hilary (1952–)
  43, 98, 141
Márquez, Gabriel García
  (1927–2014) 35, 145
Martin, George R.R. (1948–)
  147
McEwan, Ian (1948–) 22
Melville, Herman (1819–91)
  155
Mitchell, David (1969–)
  41, 94–5, 184
Moore, Lorrie (1957–) 47
Munro, Alice (1931–) 127
Murakami, Haruki (1949–)
  46, 102

Nabokov, Vladimir (1899–1977)
  173–4
Nin, Anaïs (1903–77) 23

O'Connor, Flannery (1925–64)
  69
Oates, Joyce Carol (1938–) 76
Orwell, George (1903–50)
  18–21, 185

Pamuk, Orhan (1952–) 40, 123
Perrotta, Tom (1961–) 48, 78
Picoult, Jodi (1966–) 59
Poe, Edgar Allan (1809–49) 167
Pratchett, Terry (1948–2015) 194
Priestley, J.B. (1894–1984) 141
Pullman, Philip (1946–) 124

Rhys, Jean (1890–1979) 31
Roth, Philip (1933–) 103
Rowling, J.K. (1965–) 45

Salter, James (1925–2015) 47
Sartre, Jean-Paul (1905–80)
  13
Scott, Walter (1771–1832)
  54–5, 154
Self, Will (1961–) 83
Shaw, George Bernard
  (1856–1950) 168
Shelley, Mary (1797–1851) 23
Shriver, Lionel (1957–) 138–40
Simenon, Georges (1903–89)
  75
Smith, Zadie (1975–) 85
Spark, Muriel (1918–2006)
  75, 187
Stamm, Peter (1963–) 195
Steinbeck, John (1902–68)
  105, 211
Sterne, Laurence (1713–68)
  188
Stevenson, Robert Louis
  (1850–94) 166
Stine, R.L., (1943–) 43

Swift, Jonathan (1667–1745)
  175

Tan, Amy (1952–) 107, 121
Tennant, Emma (1937–2017) 93
Thackeray, William Makepeace
  (1811–63) 168
Thoreau, Henry David (1817–62)
  14, 56
Tolstoy, Leo (1828–1910) 53, 165
Trollope, Anthony (1815–82)
  52, 113
Twain, Mark (1835–1910) 11, 164

Updike, John (1932–2009) 156

Vidal, Gore (1925–2012) 119
Vonnegut, Kurt (1922–2007) 221

Wallace, David Foster (1962–2008)
  40, 88, 203
Weldon, Fay (1931–) 77
Wells, H.G. (1866–1946) 72, 143
Wharton, Edith (1862–1937) 136
White, T.H. (1906–64) 30
Wilde, Oscar (1854–1900)
  167, 209
Williams, Joy (1944–) 200
Winton, Tim (1960–) 123
Wodehouse, P.G. (1881–1975) 109
Woolf, Virginia (1882–1941)
  118, 222

Subject index

adjectives 77, 161, 164
adverbs 162
advertising 29, 48
agents 41, 147
alcohol 42, 46, 53, 66, 70, 92, 106
Aristophanes 19
art of writing 152–205
audience 54–5, 84, 105, 126, 161,
    213, *see also* readers
Austen, Jane 173
automatic writing 13

bad writers 118, 119, 170
becoming a writer 8–49
beginning 65, 75, 83, 89, 98, 103,
    109, 133, 145
Berlin 42
Berry, Walter 136
Blake, William 18
blank pages 7, 67, 150, 204
bookshops 62, 150
boredom 83, 119, 192, 215
Bradbury, Malcolm 62
breakfast 52, 60, 66
Brooke, Rupert 27

Carver, Raymond 97
Catholicism 31
cats 19, 75, 151
characters 13, 65, 68, 82, 83, 89, 93,
    98, 103, 115, 127, 148, 151, 159, 166,
    176, 177, 180–2, 184, 186
Chekhov, Anton 97, 192
Chesterton, G.K. 194
childhood 15, 18, 23, 31, 32, 39, 40,
    85, 134, 135, 184
children 6, 15, 59, 92, 210
Christie, Agatha 180–1
coffee 49, 52, 66, 78, 88
computers 6, 83, 85, 86, 94, 220
Conan Doyle, Arthur 180–1, 217

concentration 75, 80, 88, 89, 94,
    102, 191
criticism 53, 129, 136
cutting 127, 145, 151, 171, 185

deadlines 147, 148, 220
death 15, 21, 158, 180, 210, 211, 213,
    215, 220
depression 86, 127
description 19, 20, 26, 162, 174
desks 26, 66, 75, 82, 83, 88, 101,
    108–9, 120, 123, 131, 132, 192
detective stories 180–3
dialect 162, 166
dialogue 26, 91, 98, 105, 161, 222
Dick, Philip K. 86
Dickens, Charles 173
discipline 20, 59, 94, 100, 196, 208
Dostoevsky, Fyodor 53
draft, first 78, 91, 142, 196
dreams 23, 61, 70, 83, 156
Dublin 62

editors 7, 11, 28, 29, 36, 92, 128, 147,
    156
Ellison, Ralph 131

failing 47, 110–51
fantasy 194
fathers 12, 18, 42, 117, 202
Faulkner, William 191
finishing 63, 206–22
Freeman, Austin 181–2

Gilbert & Sullivan 26
Glyn, Elinor 48
grammar 70, 135, 168, 201
Greene, Graham 77

haiku 47
happiness 11, 28, 31, 67, 114

happy ending 209, 218
Harry Potter 45
Hazlitt, William 166
health and sickness 27, 55, 75, 131
Hemingway, Ernest 48, 106, 191
Herodotus 66

imitation 10, 13, 19, 23, 96, 182
Internet 6, 41, 85, 86, 89, 94
Irving, John 191

James, Henry 193
Japan 41, 46
jargon 185
Johnson, Samuel 213
journalists 19, 21, 28, 147

Kafka, Franz 35
Koestler, Arthur 84

London 7, 41, 45, 49, 194
loneliness 15, 18, 22, 35, 69, 82
lunch 15, 66

magazines 11, 19, 36, 39, 48, 58
manuscripts 11, 28, 91, 128, 158, 220
metaphors 136, 185
methods and means 50–109
Milton, John 20
money 20, 48, 54–5, 184
Moorcock, Michael 93
mornings 6, 58, 60, 62, 66, 71, 78, 86,
    88, 101, 127, 131
mothers 15, 18, 42, 47, 86, 134
music 86, 101, 102, 124, 141

Nabokov, Vladimir 86
narrative 6, 89, 98, 158, 159, 161, 174,
    191, 194, 196, 201, 204, *see also* plot
New York 28, 101
Nigeria 39

noise 66
note cards 86, 98, 191–2
notebooks 13, 15, 83, 91

O'Connor, Flannery 191
originality 10, 11, 13, 28, 195

painting 171, 195
Paris 108
patience 84, 129, 141, 191, 198
pens 6, 45, 52, 58, 77, 78, 91
plagiarism 13, 18
planning 62, 65, 68, 107, 167, 168
plays 19, 59, 216
plot 41, 128, 167, 186, 215, *see also*
   narrative
Poe, Edgar Allen 97, 180
poetry 18, 19, 22, 27, 29, 39, 66, 70,
   93, 122, 154, 167, 173, 191, 192, 193
poets 10, 27, 49, 122, 154
politics 21, 122
praise 36, 47, 48, 157
prizes 138
procrastination 54, 56
protagonist 122, 210
Proust, Marcel 70, 120
psychoanalysis 31
publishers 28, 39, 41, 43, 94–5, 120,
   121, 129, 138, 147, 168, 194
punctuation 162, 167, 220

readers 102, 105, 126, 138, 145, 156,
   158, 159, 162, 166, 169, 171, 173,
   174, 177, 180–3, 187, 189, 192–3,
   194, 203, 216, 217
reading 22, 40, 42, 76, 85, 87, 96–7,
   135
realism 160, 181, 187, 193
regret 150, 151, 217
rejection 29, 36, 41
repetition 136

rereading 52, 91, 181
reviews 92, 120, 138, 156
rewriting 11, 28, 72, 78, 101, 105,
   120, 142, 147, 150, 162, 208, 220
rhythm 21, 105, 201
Rousseau, Jean-Jacques 53
rules 85, 92, 96–7, 105, 141, 157, 162,
   170, 174, 180–3, 185, 194, 220

school 18, 19, 26, 42, 59, 134
science fiction 36, 93
scientists 10, 13, 21, 189
self-help books 138
sentences 13, 36, 49, 68, 85, 119, 120,
   164, 193, 200, 201, 203
sex 35, 184
Shakespeare, William 76, 166
Sherlock Holmes 169, 213, 217
short stories 13, 18, 35, 36, 37, 41, 58,
   96, 129, 131, 192–3, 200
similes 20, 28, 185
slang 58, 168
smoking 26, 28, 53, 66
Somerset Mauham, William 31
spelling 20, 91
Stein, Gertude 10
subject matter 155
success 119–20, 138–40
Swinburne, Algernon Charles 27
syntax 70, 136, 201

talent 10, 36, 48, 120, 132, 154, 175,
   181, 191, 198, 203
tea 6, 66, 86
teachers 41, 47, 62, 86, 107, 173
timekeeping 6, 52, 59, 66, 88
Tolstoy, Leo 112
tricks 60, 101, 180, 192
typewriting 6, 28, 70, 72, 77, 80, 83,
   88, 91, 103, 134, 220
typography 21

university/college 26–7, 34, 62

walking 46, 53, 60, 66, 74, 101, 109,
   141
war 18, 27, 28, 42, 187
wisdom 14, 68, 178
word counts 52, 60, 72, 100
words 34, 91, 98, 120, 156, 162, 169,
   185, 201
world building 194
writer's block 59, 114, 119, 124, 137,
   142, 145, 146, 148
writing
   badly 142, 146, 202
   at night 28, 53, 58, 61, 67, 86, 101,
   132
   quickly 11, 17, 49, 54, 105, 208
   regularly 52, 62, 75, 86–7
   simply 164, 171, 182

Acknowledgements

Various publishers, individuals and estates have generously given permission to use extracts from the following copyright works.

Paul Beatty, 'My working day: "I've got no idea how winning is going to affect my writing life, but I'm going to find out."' copyright © Guardian News & Media Ltd 2017.

Roald Dahl interview with Todd McCormack reprinted with the permission of David Higham Associates Ltd.

Joe Dunthorne, interview with Tom Seymour reprinted with the permission of Tom Seymour.

Elena Ferrante, 'Women of 2015: Elena Ferrante, writer' by Liz Jobey, FT Magazine, FT.com, 11 December 2015. Used under licence from the Financial Times. All rights reserved.

Richard Ford, 'Ten Rules for Writing Fiction' reprinted with permission of ICM Partners. All rights reserved.

Jonathan Franzen, 'Modern life has become extremely distracting' copyright © Guardian News & Media Ltd 2017.

Jonathan Franzen, 'Writer's Toolbox' courtesy of Gotham Writers: www.GothamWriters.com

Graham Greene, *Ways of Escape* courtesy of David Higham Associates Ltd.

Helle Helle, interview courtesy of Cara Benson and Bookslut: www.bookslut.com

Ernest Hemingway, *By-Line: Ernest Hemingway*, edited by William White. Copyright © 1967 by By-Line Ernest Hemingway Copyright renewed © 1995 by Patrick Hemingway and John H. Hemingway. Reprinted with the permission of Scribner, a Division of Simon & Schuster, Inc. All rights reserved.

Ernest Hemingway, *Ernest Hemingway, Selected Letters 1917–1961*, edited by Carlos Baker. Copyright © 1967 by By-Line Ernest Hemingway. Copyright renewed © 1995 by Patrick Hemingway and John H. Hemingway. Reprinted with the permission of Scribner, a Division of Simon & Schuster, Inc. All rights reserved.

Han Kang, 'Violence and Being Human: A Conversation with Han Kang by Krys Lee' courtesy of *World Literature Today*.

Deborah Levy, *Things I don't want to know* reprinted with the permission of The Wylie Agency (UK) Ltd.

C.S. Lewis, *Surprised by Joy: The Shape of My Early Life* copyright © C.S. Lewis Pte. Ltd. 1955. Extract reprinted by permission.

Toby Litt, 'Sport – or, What Can Writers Learn From Athletes and Coaches' reprinted with the permission of Curtis Brown Ltd.

Hilary Mantel, 'Hilary Mantel's rules for writers' copyright © Guardian News & Media Ltd 2017.

George R.R. Martin, 'Last Year (Winds of Winter)' copyright © George R.R. Martin 2016. Published by permission of George R.R. Martin c/o The Lotts Agency, Ltd.

David Mitchell, interview courtesy of Chris Park and Northern Soul webzine: www.northernsoul.me.uk

Anais Nin, *The Diary of Anais Nin, Volume Five: 1947–1955* copyright © 1974 by Anais Nin. Used by permission of Houghton Mifflin Harcourt Publishing Company. All rights reserved.

Joyce Carol Oates, 'Letter to a Fiction Writer' reprinted by permission of John Hawkins and Associates, Inc. Copyright © 1999 The Ontario Review.

Flannery O'Connor, 'The Regional Writer' courtesy of *Esprit* magazine.

James Salter, 'Some for Glory, Some for Praise' reprinted with permission of ICM Partners. All rights reserved.

Will Self, 'Review: Writers' rooms: Will Self' copyright © Guardian News & Media Ltd 2017.

Zadie Smith, 'Zadie Smith's Rules for Writers'. Published by The Guardian 2010. Copyright © Zadie Smith. Reproduced by permission of the author c/o Rogers, Coleridge & White Ltd., 20 Powis Mews, London W11 1JN.

Muriel Spark, *Loitering With Intent* courtesy of David Higham Associates Ltd.

T.H. White, *England Have My Bones* courtesy of David Higham Associates Ltd.

Tim Winton, 'A Life in Books' copyright © Guardian News & Media Ltd 2017.

Thanks

We would both like to thank everyone at Frances Lincoln
for their tireless work in guiding this book from proposal
to print. This book was only possible with the help of
numerous writers, publishers, agents, executors and estates.
Thank you all. A special thanks also goes to Emily Bick and
Jonathan Paul.

Being a Writer

© 2017 Quarto Publishing plc

Selection and introduction
© 2017 Travis Elborough and Helen Gordon
Illustrations © 2017 Joey Guidone
Design: Glenn Howard
Editor: Michael Brunström
Commissioning editor: Zena Alkayat

First Published in 2017 by Frances Lincoln,
an imprint of The Quarto Group.
The Old Brewery, 6 Blundell Street,
London N7 9BH, United Kingdom.
T (0)20 7700 6700 **F** (0)20 7700 8066
www.QuartoKnows.com

A catalogue record for this book is available from the British Library.

ISBN 978-0-7112-3820-6

Printed and bound in China

9 8 7 6 5 4 3 2 1